Beyond the Culture Tours:

Studies in Teaching and Learning With Culturally Diverse Texts

Beyond the Culture Tours:

Studies in Teaching and Learning With Culturally Diverse Texts

Gladys Cruz

Sarah Jordan

José Meléndez

Steven Ostrowski

Alan C. Purves

LEA LAWRENCE ERLBAUM ASSOCIATES, PUBLISHERS

1997 **Mahwah, New Jersey** **London**

Lawrence Erlbaum Associates, Inc., Publishers
10 Industrial Avenue
Mahwah, NJ 07430

Library of Congress Cataloging-in-Publication Data

Beyond the culture tours : studies in teaching and learning with culturally diverse texts / Gladys Cruz ... [et al.].
    p. cm.
Includes bibliographical references (p.).
ISBN 0-8058-2612-2 (c : alk. paper). — ISBN 0-8058-2613-0 (p : alk. paper)
    1. Literature—Study and teaching (Secondary)   2. Literature, Comparative—Study and Teaching (Secondary)   3. Multiculturalism—Study and Teaching (Secondary)   4. Pluralism (Social science) in literature. I. Cruz, Gladys, 1961–
    PN59. B46 1997
    807'.1'273—dc21   97–955
                                      CIP

Books published by Lawrence Erlbaum Associates are printed on acid-free paper and their bindings are chosen for strength and durability

Printed in the United States of America
10 9 8 7 6 5 4 3 2 1

In memory of Alan C. Purves

It is only fitting that one of his last books be about
exploring how we learn about each other

Contents

Preface

This volume represents the result of four years' work on the study and teaching of multicultural literature undertaken from 1991 to 1995 by a research team from the National Center for Research in the Learning and Teaching of Literature. The study team included faculty and graduate students at The University at Albany, State University of New York, and a number of teachers in secondary schools across the United States.

There are several premises underlying the study. One of the major issues in literature education today is that of multiculturalism and its relation to the general goals of teaching critical thinking in and through literature (Ravitch, 1990a, 1990b). This issue becomes particularly salient when one considers the transitions of various cultural minorities into the mainstream of American society and education. A general approach to literature education "for all" may serve to undermine the existing cultures of the society and move our society willy-nilly into a standardization without cultural identity. At the same time there is the charge that overemphasis on the particular culture from which the students come will foster separatism and even racism. Either extreme can lead to strife both within the schools and without, as has been seen in various societies around the world.

Culture should be regarded as a direct source of inspiration for development, and in return, development should assign to culture a central role as a social regulator. This imperative applies not only to developing countries, where economic extroversion and cultural alienation have clearly and sometimes dramatically widened the gap between the creative and productive processes. It is also increasingly vital for industrialized countries, where the headlong race for growth in material wealth is detrimental to the spiritual, ethical and aesthetic aspects of life, and creates much disharmony between man and the natural environment. (Mayor, 1988, p. 5)

The thrust of such a statement for educational research in the United States, with its large numbers of native and immigrant minorities, is that to see education as solely the training of critical thinking may lead people away from their past and their family; and can cause alienation as well as acculturation. At the same time, ethnic studies for members of particular ethnic groups without any attention to the broader culture may harm the fabric of our society. Research may help make it possible to determine which educational programs serve best to educate people for intellectual development without destroying their cultural heritage and cultural pride, and which programs may best serve to show the diverse strength of our pluralistic society.

Much of the attention to the complex issue of cultural literacy and multiculturalism in literature learning has focused on the culture of the texts offered in the curriculum. This attention has raised as a major issue representation by writers from ethnic minorities or women writers. It is important that curriculum planning address such issues as fairness in the schools, but to focus only on these issues when studying cultural variation is to see only one half of the picture. One must also consider the issue of teachers and students from one culture reading and responding to works from other cultures. What distinctive characteristics of reading and response exist for such students? How are the aims of multicultural teaching of literature accomplished? How should a teacher deal with the cultural differences of readers? These were the central questions of the project.

As a first stage in the study, a conference was called in the spring of 1991 to discuss the issues of multiculturalism and literature in the broader context of literacy. Organized by Alan Purves along with Professors Suzanne Miller and Barbara McCaskill, the conference brought together poets, novelists, theorists, critics, and teachers for a 3-day discussion of the issues. The results of this conference have been published in *Multicultural Literature: Making Space for Difference* (Miller & MacCaskill, 1993). That volume raised a number of issues concerning the culture of the writer and how the work reflected or rubbed against that culture; how the critic and the curriculum might think of the text in a multicultural perspective, and the implications for selection and presentation of texts; and the role of the teacher in presenting works from cultures other than his or her own to students who might share cultures with neither the teacher nor the text.

With the perspective of that conference in their minds, the team then decided to explore some of the questions raised by the conference participants, and to do so in a dual fashion, first by examining how students approached texts that came from either their culture or another, and second by analyzing how teachers perceived the students, the literature, and their role. The questions were related, but the investigations were somewhat distinct in that different groups of teachers and students were approached in different phases of the study. The team and the set of questions and issues were held in common.

Chapter 1, by Alan C. Purves, offers an overview of the project. The ensuing chapters detail the various aspects of the study. In chapter 2, Sarah Jordan reports the results of two studies examining how students react to texts from outside their own culture. The first study was based on in-depth interviews with students, and the second on a national survey. For the first study, researchers asked students to read several texts and comment on what information was needed for the text to make more sense to the student. The results of this study are written up with a focus on comments made by students, comments that were used to pinpoint specific problem areas. One of the most frequent responses was that the problem was not a lack of information, but instead a reading deficiency on the part of the student or the difficulty of the text.

Because it was much larger, data from the second study are presented as trends. After reading a text, students were given a list of questions that could be asked about the story or poem, and asked to pick the three most important questions that could be asked about the text. Students were also asked to describe the culture of the text and rate that culture on a set of 5-point scales. These responses were also analyzed to find if there was any interaction between the culture of the text and the culture of the student.

The final part of chapter 2 is a review of what these studies have revealed about students and multicultural texts. This part of the chapter is structured with headings that read, "What do we know? We know. . . ."

In chapter 3, a more detailed study of the exposure a small number of readers from Puerto Rico and the Dominican Republic to prose and poetry from writers of diverse ethnic backgrounds, Gladys Cruz analyzes responses of the students in light of the cultures of the students and the texts. Students' ideas and preferences in how literature should be presented in the classroom were also explored. The results suggest a diversity within ethnic groups often classified under umbrella terms such as *Hispanic, Asian, White,* and the like.

In chapter 4, Steven Ostrowski takes a close look at 25 English and language arts teachers from around the United States who use multicultural literature in their classrooms. The issues he explores include how teachers locate and choose appropriate multicultural literature, their goals, the various methodologies they employ, and their perceptions of how their own students respond to the literature they are being asked to study. Based on hundreds of pages of correspondence and conversations with the 25 teachers, Ostrowski describes the problems and successes of people who are doing what might very well be called pioneering work in literature studies in United States secondary schools. Fundamental problems include the fact that many teachers are unsure of just what constitutes a "culture." They are also often unsure whether or not a given text is "representative" of a given culture. Although teachers' goals tend toward the demonstration to students that, despite certain differences, all people and cultures share important similarities, students sometimes resist. "Why do we need to know about them?" and "What have they got to do with me?" are not uncommon student responses to attempts at teaching the literature of the "other." However, there also are triumphs. For instance, a number of teachers spoke of the empathy students came to feel toward people and cultures they previously disliked or failed to understand after having studied a piece of cultural literature.

Finally, in chapter 5, José Meléndez explores the theoretical issues in multicultural literature teaching. As the previous chapters have noted, there exists a lack of clarity about the nature of the study of culture and literature and the purposes and practices in presenting them to students. This chapter seeks to provide a theoretical grounding for good practice. These concepts involve the nature of the writer, the locus of the literary text, the cultural forces that impinge on the reader in the act of reading, and the culture of the classroom—where many of the oral and written responses to a text take place. Finally, the chapter explores the pedagogical issues surrounding the themes of universality and particularity in literature and response to literature.

In any study such as this, there are a number of people to thank. First of all there were the organizers and participants in the 1991 conference mentioned previously. They helped set the agenda for the studies as well as influence the thinking and observations of the participants. Second, there were a number of research assistants and staff who helped in various stages of the project: Elba Herrera, Godfrey Rivera, Nancy Michelson, Kathleen Sims, and Caryn Francis. Shouming Li helped immeasurably by preparing the statistical analyses for chapter 2. Ellen Mainwaring and Linda Papa coped with much of the logistical support, aided by a small army of work-study students. James Peltz aided in editing material throughout the course of the study.

Above all, we are grateful to the students and teachers who contributed their time and energy over 3 years to helping us in our research. For the most part, the students remained anonymous; the teachers, however, did not, and we acknowledge them here: *California*: Site Coordinator: Will Lindwall, English Language Arts Specialist, San Diego City School District; Teachers: Gloria Lewis and Amy C. Wilkerson, Serra High School. *Hawaii*: Site Coordinator: Kathleen Dudden Andrasick; Teachers Lori Hamel, Maydeen T. Minami, Roosevelt High School; Jan M. K. Kanacholo, Waipahu High School. *Kansas*: Site Coordinators: Bryant Fillion and Tonya Huber, Wichita State University; Teachers: Norma Couchman, Linda Hoobler, Northeast Magnet High School; Stacie Valdez and Gayle Jackson, Wichita North High School; Myrna Steele, Wichita East High School. *Montana*: Site Coordinator: Beverly Chin, University of Montana; Teachers: Margaret Abbott, Poplar High School; Donna Miller, Chinook High School; Timothy Marchant, St. Ignatius High School; Laurie Nelson, Hardin High School; Katy Paynich, Bozeman High School; Dorothea Susag, Simms High School. *New Jersey*: Site Coordinator: Willa Spicer; Teachers: Barbara King-Shaver, Joyce Greenberg Lott, Mark Zaminski, South Brunswick High School. *New York*: Site Coordinator: Philip Anderson, Queens College; Teachers: Mary E. Carter and Judith Maltz, Newtown High School; Doris Sachs and Daniel T. Smith, Richmond Hill High School. Finally, we want to thank Naomi Silverman and Linda Henigin for their assistance in seeing this book through publication, and the various reviewers whose comments helped make the book both readable, and, we hope, helpful to educational planners and teachers.

1

Introduction: The Grand Tour and Other Forays

Alan C. Purves

In calling this book *Beyond the Culture Tours*, we wanted to bring the reader's attention to a set of issues in the teaching of literature and culture. The Culture Tour is an old concept in the West, dating back certainly to the 17th century. The educated young man (it was an exclusively male project at first) was expected to round off his education with the Grand Tour. This meant a visit to the major sites on the European continent, particularly those associated with Greece and Rome. Some also traveled to the Holy Land. The object was to have a first-hand view of these monuments, and looking at them alone brought people the reputation of being cultured or well traveled. The idea of the Grand Tour extended into the 19th and 20th centuries, particularly for Americans who believed it educational to travel to England and the Continent (there was only one "continent" that counted).

As the idea spread in the early part of the 20th century, it allowed for the vicarious tour rather than the actual one. Students were asked to look at collections or reproductions of art works, listen to concerts or later recordings, and read certain "classical" works drawn from what has come to be known as the *canon*. The point of this form of education was that exposure to these works in itself formed a version of the Grand Tour, and was sufficient. If one did not go to colleges where this form of education was offered, one could do it oneself by buying Dr. Eliot's *Five-Foot Shelf* of classic books or some other compendium of culture.

As Americans rediscovered the variety of their culture in the 1930s and beyond, they became aware of the importance of the folk cultures, both regional and ethnic. Compendia of these regional cultures were gathered and edited for consumption. In the burgeoning of ethnic and feminist awareness in the 1960s and 1970s, there arose anthologies and courses that adapted the idea of the Grand Tour to the newly found subgroups. It was possible to read a book by Richard Wright and a couple of poems by Langston Hughes and thus "know" the African American culture. One could gain similar "knowledge" of the feminist culture by reading Sarah Orne Jewett and Susan Glaspell.

1

The basic idea behind the tour approach is that exposure to a culture in books is like travel to an ethnic theme park. School and college courses have the look of Afram Disney World or Post-Colonial Latinosburg. By taking such a course one is a tourist in the culture and can therefore appreciate it. Such courses often retain a sense of the opposition of colorful "folk cultures" to the main culture of the Western European and particularly Greco-Roman that persists from the earlier approach. As Simon Schama (1989) pointed out, the idea of the "folk" culture has been seen as oppositional to the Greco-Roman culture for more than 1500 years, but it has seldom sought to replace what is ingrained as the truly central culture of the Classical Age. The tour approach to the study of a culture still prevails in the thinking of many educators and curriculum planners; it is popular with booksellers as well.

The approach has been challenged by many people, however, because it is superficial. It fails to deal with some of the issues of attitude and approach to culture and cultures that some believe should be addressed. If one remains the tourist—the observer—one is looking at the culture from the outside. The tourist remains distant, perhaps superior, safe in a cocoon of ethnocentrism.

Two alternate approaches seem to have emerged to counter the touristic approach. The first is what might be called the "bazaar approach." In the bazaar is the mingling of a variety of peoples with their goods and wares. The bazaar is the meeting place, the agora or caravansary. In it each group may be distinct, but there is a curious melding. Today, the bazaar is represented by the food court in a mall. The bazaar approach is based on the idea of "one world," or of universality, a theme that has captivated scholars in many fields and has dominated the modernist and positivist approaches to the social sciences. Those who have studied folklore have found common themes across the cultures of the world. They have looked for the single theme or set of themes that bring all peoples together. Some have gone to the Freudian or the Jungian schools of psychology, and to the concept of the archetype, to find those themes that appear to cut across all the various cultures. Such a view tends to flatten out differences; for example, all cultures consider the moon to be a feminine symbol (if a culture does not it is simply omitted from the archetype study as an inconvenience).

The bazaar approach has its advocates in those who adopt the thematic approaches to literature and attempt to find connections among peoples. Several of the teachers from the project focus on this way of looking at literature and culture. They find that it is a good way to help students explore their own interconnections as well, particularly in a class where people from different cultural backgrounds may be congregated. When looking at the literature of the United States in particular, the traditional metaphor of the melting pot, with its stress on connections, can be useful, but it can also lead to a false sense of unity. When one looks only at the similarities, one ignores those features that make a culture distinct.

The second alternative is the student-of-culture approach, or the "young anthropologist." I would not use the term *cultural studies*, because that label is often associated with various versions of Marxism. In the student-of-culture approach to the literature of various cultures, the major premise holds that texts come from writers who inhabit cultural contexts that shape their writing. The text is simultaneously an individual aesthetic object and a cultural document, a part of the legacy of an individual and a group. The literature of a country is the literature of men and women of all sorts of subcultures—racial, ethnic, national, regional, local, and personal.

Such texts are to be read not as disembodied from their creators, but as intimate parts of their culture. Reading the text is to read it in the light of what Hazlitt called the "spirit of the age," or of the culture from which it comes. The student is to try to understand the work in terms of what it meant at the time of its writing, as well as its implications for the reader today. That Shakespeare "writ not for an age but for all time" must be rethought as "Shakespeare wrote both for an age and for all time." The same can be applied to modern authors, such as Chinua Achebe and Margaret Atwood.

The students of culture start from the premise that as with other pieces of art, literary texts have creators who inhabit and half-create the various cultures of the world. If students remember that simple fact, then they have reinstated the author and they see that texts come from a context that is rich and complex, and can best be understood within that context. As students read the text they build up their knowledge of that context, and they also use that context to help further read and comprehend the text. They are not to be ignorant but clever readers relying on their own wits to come up with the ingenious interpretation, they are readers who strive to be more fully aware of the writer's world and the text's relation to that world. They make connections among texts, build their canons, and examine the mosaic of cultures that constitute their world.

What is important in the curriculum, particularly at the secondary level, is to provide a broad variety of texts from around the world. Such a view is that of Northrop Frye (1957), who held that all works of literature are to be held as equally valid, and that it is not the role of criticism or the schools to rank them. In one of his last writings, he summarized his definition of literature:

> where the organizing principles are myth, that is, story or narrative, and metaphor, that is, figured language. Here we are in a completely liberal world, the world of the free movement of the spirit. If we read a story there is no pressure to believe in it or act upon it; if we encounter metaphors in poetry, we need not worry about their factual absurdity. Literature incorporates our ideological concerns, but it devotes itself mainly to the primary ones, in both physical and spiritual forms: its fictions show human beings in the primary throes of surviving, loving, prospering, and fighting with the frustrations that block those things. It is at once a world of relaxation, where even the most terrible tragedies are still called plays, and a world of far greater intensity than ordinary life affords. In short it does everything that can be done for people except transform them. It creates a world that the spirit can live in, but it does not make us spiritual beings. (Frye, 1991, p. 16)

In taking such a definition, students see that an individual work is a part of the totality of myth; at the same time, it is situated in the world from which it came. The students can come to understand both aspects, and they can also come to explore their own responses to the work as outsiders and as anthropologists seeking to be inside.

In transforming this double vision to the curriculum, we recognize the pressures of the world in which teachers and students reside. To be sure, there must be constraints to ensure a breadth of selection from the totality of literature—Sappho to Narayan; tales of the First Nations of this continent to those of Stan Lee, Harper

Lee, and Spike Lee. These works might be grouped at times by the cultures of the authors, but at other times texts from disparate cultures might be yoked so that they can be compared and contrasted. Both groupings help students learn to look at texts as individual worlds of the larger universe of myth and metaphor, and as written by people who have real lives and real backgrounds, and who express their culture in manifold ways be it a mainstream culture or a marginalized culture, or a culture of race, gender, sexuality, or physical difference. We can read John Milton's poetry as the work of an Englishman, a defeated and disgraced Protestant radical, a man, and a blind person. All of these additions to our knowledge help us to see a work like *Samson Agonistes* more clearly than if we treated it as being written anonymously. But we cannot forget it is also part of the larger matrix of drama. We can make the same claim about Gwendolyn Brooks: American, African American, woman, urbanite, midwesterner, caught up in the Civil Rights movement of the 1960s in both the South and Chicago and its suburbs (e.g., Cicero). To know these facets of the poet is to help us read "The Ballad of Rudolph Reed." But we must also read it as a ballad, a poetic object.

In her spiritual autobiography *Encountering God: From Bozeman to Benares* (1993) the theologian Diana Eck discussed the issue of the many religions of the world, and the responses of any one religion to that multiplicity. She described three approaches that have been taken. The first approach is exclusionist, in which the members of one religion assert that theirs is the only true religion and all the others are false; the second is inclusionist, which accepts the partial truth of all and tries to fit them into the one religion to which the apologists belong; the third approach is pluralism, which accepts the parallel existence of different religions and seeks to establish both points of contact and points of difference.

The same tripartite argument can be applied to the issue of cultural variety and the variety of literatures in the United States and the world in our metaphors of the tour, the bazaar, and the student of culture. The exclusionist approach to culture is well summed up in the work of William Bennett and others who assert that the "Western Culture" based on the Judeo-Greek tradition of Europe is the only culture worth knowing and is the culture that has remained somewhat pure and untainted by foreign influence. Whether true or not (and the "tainting" has been apparent from the very beginning of the "Western Tradition," when Herodotus explored and brought back ideas from other worlds), the idea is powerful and one that was common in academic circles from the beginning of the 20th century and reached back to the 19th century and Matthew Arnold's *Culture and Anarchy*. It is best known through a process of reading and absorption. It is popular today with many because it is ingrained through the schools, it is convenient and relatively compact, and it allows for a strong sense of continuity.

The second, or inclusionist, view is the one that permeates the metaphors of the melting pot and the salad bowl as well as the image of the United States as the harbor of lost souls. People come from other cultures to the United States, and they bring something of that culture to this country and enrich it and broaden it, but at the same time become domesticated into the broader American picture. It is a model of culture that is shared by other countries, notably China, France, and England, each of which has absorbed peripheral cultures into a common heritage and particularly a common language. English has accepted loan words like *tobacco*, *squash*, and *verandah*; American literature has accepted the prose and poetry of

Native Americans, African Americans, and some European immigrants, particularly the Eastern European Jews. They have tended to domesticate them, however, and make them part of a unified view of the culture. Such is the view of E. D. Hirsch, Jr., James Banks, and several other writers on multiculturalism. The last sentence might strike some as a curious juxtaposition, but these writers agree on the broad principle that the culture of the United States is to be considered a bringing together of many into one. Their primary disagreement concerns the relative proportions of the Anglo-European culture to those of the other groups. The inclusionist view of culture parallels the view of Joseph Campbell's monomyth and of various followers of Jung who seek to find unity rather than diversity.

The pluralistic view is quite different. It suggests that each culture has a literature that is particular to that culture, one that arises from its particular aspirations and hurts. It is affected by place and by religion. Even when a society is displaced, the longing for the homeland permeates the thinking of the new culture. Such is a view of the many cultures of the United States that assert their independence and their connections to their roots rather than to the new land. Influenced by the strange and the new, the writers seek to retain what is theirs by heritage, not assimilation. When we approach the literatures of these cultures, we look to the differences between cultures rather than the ties across them. The ties are often so vague—like the family—that they lose any distinctive meaning when seen in the light of the African American family, the Dominican family, the Japanese family, or the Vietnamese family.

We should not pride ourselves in thinking that the pluralist view is modern or, even better, postmodern. It is an idea that lies at the very heart of comparative studies in literature and religion. Over the centuries, pluralists have argued with exclusionists or inclusionists in matters of culture and religion. Such was the case in both Alexander's and Caesar's empires, as well as in the division of Christianity between East and West. In his 1873 lecture, the great comparative linguist and folklorist F. Max Muller argued that it was precisely in rubbing edges between cultures that the most interesting thinkers and the greatest advances in cultural understanding might be made.

Each of the three views is, of course, an abstraction of the complex reality that is society. Any one person in the world is simultaneously a part of a particular culture and a part of a broader one. In the United States, there exists a general (and to the outsider, myopic) view that we are Americans and share something we perceive as American cultural values. At the same time each of us sees ourself as participating in a subset of that American general culture. This dual vision parallels the dual vision of literature described by Frye. It is indeed a difficult vision to teach, a balance to be carefully maintained.

The studies reported in this volume tend to show that most of the teachers in our study hold to the bazaar or inclusionist view of multiculturalism. Whether it is a strongly held positive belief or a default view of the culture held in the textbooks and the curriculum guides is unclear. The inclusionists make room for the new, grudgingly at times, because it is hard to get rid of the old, but there is always room for one more story, one more culture, if we can Americanize it and not make it too different.

The students in this study have, if any view, the exclusionist one. Their concerns are not with culture but with survival in school reading. When cultural issues are raised, they appear to be viewed with suspicion and with resentment about the new. Often they can accept the new in popular culture, but not so easily in the official culture that is studied in school.

What view should we take? How should we help teachers? That is the set of questions that Meléndez takes up in the last chapter. Basically, we subscribe to the third view, that of pluralism and the study of culture, not simply the relegating of culture to the theme park of the school or the mind. It is not an easy approach. It requires work on the part of students and teachers, but it is one that respects the author, the culture, and the student.

HOW LITERATURE INSTRUCTION MAKES THE TEACHING OF MULTICULTURAL LITERATURE PROBLEMATIC

A hundred years ago, literature was taught as a branch of history, either political and cultural history or philology and the history of the language through its art. The work of literature was assumed to have come from an author who lived somewhere at some time and used the language appropriate to his or her time. The literature read was assumed to have a continuity and perhaps an evolution or development toward the modern. Literature in the West sprang from the fountainheads of Israel, Greece, and Rome. When people began to write in the European vernaculars, their works were seen in relationship to these three fountainheads and certain works, particularly the Italian, Spanish, French, and English, formed the mainstream. During this time, of course, literature was intimately tied to the idea of culture. The works of literature could serve as beacons of our culture, and reading and knowing them in their cultural context could bring readers into a common fold.

For a variety of reasons, the historical and philological view of literature pedagogy began to be challenged in the 1920s. The challenges came from several areas: the influence of science and the scientific approach that sought to derive general laws; the new psychology, particularly behaviorism; and an interest in the idea of art for art's sake, or the work divorced from culture and history to be seen as a pure form approaching music. To study the work in this way—as a complex structure of language—allowed the critic reader to be scientific, to assert that the text was ultimately knowable as an object.

Such a focus accorded with the developing interest in reading and the science of reading and reading pedagogy, which sought to find impediments in understanding the text as treatable psychological problems in the reader. The idea of reading comprehension, something that could be measured objectively, took hold in the schools and burgeoned for the fifty years from 1925 to 1975. Students could be taught to comprehend pieces of writing, and the comprehension of texts was something that could be measured easily with multiple choice questions. Only in the mid-1960s did this idea of the psychology of reading begin to be challenged, and even then the challenges were not strong. The notion that the comprehension of a text might be something more complex than a simple readability formula or that there might be cultural issues involved in comprehension emerged very slowly.

The critique of such scientism combined with new views of psychology moved the focus of attention from the work as an object to the work as it was read, and therefore as an observed phenomenon and not as a pure phenomenon. Thus, during the period from 1920 to 1980, literary criticism and (lagging far behind it) literary pedagogy moved from an approach based on the scientific observation of the text to the scientific observation of the reader. The focus turned toward the behavior of readers, to their response (to use a nice behaviorist term). Pedagogically, reader-response teaching focused on the psychology of the reader and particularly on the emotions the text raised in the reader. This attention, for the most part, focused on the content (the theme) of the work, not on either its style or its cultural background, and little attention was focused on the cultural background of the reader.

The fact that the organisms responding to the stimulus might differ from each other as well as from some ideal "perfect reader" remained submerged until the African American and feminist movements of the 1960s. These two groups forced attention first on who wrote the work and then on who was reading the work. What happened in this country was mirrored in many other countries, as minority populations were "discovered" in Europe or as "new" countries sought to find their own literary voice. "Culture" was rediscovered throughout the period from 1960 to 1990, in part out of a fear that minority cultures and their artistic and literary heritage would be lost in the mad rush for development into the new media-dominated global village.

Thus, today we have the confluence of two perhaps contradictory trends in the teaching of literature. On the one hand is the long pedagogical tradition that views response to literature as a behavior that exists in a cultural vacuum, where the focus of attention is on the responding organism, that entity known as the *reader*, and at the same time holds on to the idea of the knowable and testable text. Texts are embodiments of themes or ideas, and their primary connection to each other is thematic. On the other hand is the trend to see literary works as emanating from a cultural ethos, so that the focus of attention is on the writer and the preservation of the cultural heritage, and on the reader's coming to understand and appreciate something of that heritage, and so come to honor the people born to the culture.

It's a confusing time, a time made more confusing because of the sloganeering of terms rather than their careful examination. *Reader response* is one banner, and *multiculturalism* is another. To take up the first one, it is true that when you or I read a poem, we somehow go from the eye to the mind and put the poem together in our heads, going on about our business of reading or not talking or going to sleep or not. We can't help doing that. We can call what we do a *response*, but the term does not mean that natural human penchant. Instead, we focus on what readers say and do in formal situations such as classrooms or what they write on examinations. In this sense *response* is a formal academic activity that has certain rules and procedures set forth by the current critical or pedagogical fashion. When we examine *response* in this light, we are looking at what the schools want readers to say or write about literary works. Generally, the textbooks and the tests remain focused on the genre and content of the work as an external object and on the emotions, thoughts, and attitudes of the reader as an individual member of a group known as "the literature student." All of these objects need to be attended to in proper rhetorical format: the response journal, the synopsis and statement of theme (particularly the "hidden" meaning), and the noting of certain literary features (the taught literary terms).

Multicultural, to take on the other term, refers to the fact that our society is a mixture. Most societies are mixtures, increasingly so because of the ease of travel and the shift of labor forces. As a counter to the trend of homogenization, there comes the desire to preserve group identity. One way to do this is to recognize the prior literary and artistic achievements of the group and establish a canon of literary works that marks knowledge of that group. A group without a canon has no existence. In the multicultural perspective, literature is not that pure aesthetic construct devoid of background; this perspective suggests that there is no such thing as "the poem," there are only poems, and they are written by people who used to or currently live and breathe. Poems come from people and poems have a history, just as people have a history.

Taken as extremes and as slogans, the two positions are mutually exclusive, and the pedagogy of literature becomes a mess. Such a set of contradictions is present in the responses of the students, who often see themselves caught up in reading comprehension and its toils. It is also present in the statements of the teachers, many of whom are in the process of sorting out the contradiction. How to resolve this mess is a complex problem, because it involves undoing a large set of ingrained habits of mind. It is hoped that this volume may, indeed, contribute to the resolution.

2

Student Responses to Culturally Diverse Texts

◈ ◆ ◈

Sarah Jordan

As Alan Purves explains in the preface, we have spent several years investigating how students respond to texts written by authors who are not of the students' culture. We wanted to see if we could pinpoint some of the problems that students encounter with such texts. We began by interviewing students and teachers about their experiences reading and teaching these texts in order to define the issues and questions to be used in a larger study (Jordan & Purves, 1993). Then we went national: Using the information, we contacted high schools across the country that had particular population distributions, and asked students to read texts and respond to questions. Both the pilot and the national studies are reported in this chapter.

The early technical reports have been rewritten, in part because of the insights offered in the next chapter, which notes that students may share nothing in common but a particular label—in this case, Hispanic. In fact, we found during the first study that labeling ethnic background proved to be problematic, because many students were of mixed racial and ethnic backgrounds. One student, for example, had been born in Korea but had been adopted by an Anglo-European family. Another student was of African American heritage but lived with her White parents. Several students described their background as mixed Native American and European. Another reason for rewriting the reports was the realization that I, as one of the authors, was writing from a particular background and was placing certain academic expectations on the students and their responses. With the help of the others, I have tried to recast these responses in a more neutral light.

THE PROBLEM OF PROBLEMS

This purpose of this study was to investigate what problems in understanding readers face when they read texts from a culture other than their own. When people read, the information in the text interacts with the information in the reader's head, and an understanding or interpretation of the text is created. A new text is an "unknown," and the reader tries to make sense of it by using prior information to fill in gaps in understanding. Understanding of and interaction with the text is shaped by many, many factors, such as the background knowledge, reading ability, and expectations of the situation in which the reading takes place.

The problems we are discussing do not refer to decoding so much as to response and criticism. In high school, decoding problems indicate learning disabilities. Most high school teachers can—and do—expect their students to show up in class with the ability to read a text and grasp its gist. And that's what students do: They read a text for its basic meaning or for its basic story. Deeper analysis depends on many factors, most generally what the students have been taught by a teacher or teachers to look for.

What we wanted to know was, given a text from a very different social, cultural, and intellectual background from that of the reader, would the "gap" between cultures create difficulties in making sense of a text different from those that inhibit readers generally? Would students be unable to get the gist of the text? We also wanted to investigate some other questions:

Do readers' criteria for judging works differ when the works are outside of their culture?
Do readers shift approaches in their discourse depending on the culture of the text?
Are different kinds of readers the products of cultural forces, or are they simply individuals within the general matrix of "the American student"?
Is the process of reader identification with the text modified by either the culture of the text or the culture of the reader?
Does the pleasure of reading a text vary depending on the distance of the text from the reader's culture?

A PRELIMINARY LOOK

To begin to see how better to shape these questions, we focused on the interviewing high school students from the following groups: African American, Asian, Native American, Hispanic/Latino, and Anglo-European. We also tried to find students involved in the area of women's studies. Students were selected from six school districts, representing two rural, three urban, and one suburban system. The students were in 10th or 11th grade and had volunteered to participate in the study. There were 89 interviews, distributed as shown in Table 2.1.

The texts were chosen to represent variations in ethnicity of author or central figure, gender of author or central figure, and locale (urban/rural). (Please see the Appendix at the end of this volume for list of texts.)

RESULTS

Student Responses

The student interviews took several forms, in part to determine which form could get the most extensive response. Because we were trying to pinpoint problems and develop questions, we didn't want to make things easy for students. Therefore, in the first interviews students were not told anything about the piece, neither its author nor its background. Without this information, however, a great deal of time was spent helping students make some connection to the text. We then presented the text as an example of literature from a particular background. Students were asked, as a prereading exercise, about preconceptions they had of this culture. For example, one student, when asked "What do you think a story from China will have?" replied, "Lanterns and women in hats." This prereading exercise opened up the possibility of being able to discuss the literature as a cultural piece. It also allowed us, as researchers and teachers, to find out a student's prior knowledge and gaps in background information about a culture.

The responses to the interview questions were analyzed according to whether they were deemed to be in the nature of background information about the culture of the text, stereotyping the culture of the text, interpreting the text, or judging the text. These categories were defined by these questions:

A. Background Information
　　1. After reading the text, how many students asked for background information on the culture?
　　2. How many supplied background information about the culture?
　　3. How many mentioned the author?

B. Stereotyping
　　1. How many rejected the text as alien?
　　2. How many showed stereotypes about the culture in their responses?

C. Interpreting
　　1. How many looked for pleasant interpretations?
　　2. How many differentiated the two texts on a cultural basis?
　　3. What misunderstandings on a cultural level occurred?

D. Judging
　　1. What were reasons for liking or disliking the text?
　　2. How many identified with the piece?

In the analysis, we looked for evidence of cultural awareness. We really wanted students to ask for information, to tell us what they needed to know in order to make more sense of a text. This was a difficult task for students. People read to understand, and they consciously or unconsciously supply information needed to

TABLE 2.1

Distribution of Participants in Preliminary Study

	Female	Male
African American	11	9
Anglo-European	45	18
Other	2	4

make sense of a text. It requires a major shift in the way that students read to ask them to explore *differences*—to look for things that they do not understand. If students don't look for differences, they may not ask for information that might help them understand a text, an idea, or another person. This is why the first set of questions focuses on how many students asked for more information.

Background Information

This group of questions deals with whether the students tended to treat the texts within a cultural context. They could do so by either asking about or supplying background cultural information. We found that almost any question could be considered a request for cultural background, although few questions were worded as specific requests. Most questions or statements about the piece were about the author of the text, a pattern that reflects the culture of the school, where students are often taught that a story (or poem) is the creation of a particular person. Students, in general, are not taught to see texts as artifacts of a particular culture and, therefore, are unable to discuss them as such.

What sorts of questions did students ask? Most wanted to know about the author. One student asked if the interviewer was the author of the piece, two wanted the "who when where what" in order for the text to make more sense or have more meaning. For example, one student said that she liked the poem "Nikki Rosa," and that she understood it. However, she wanted more information to place the author in a context. Was the author writing about a project in Chicago, or was the poem placed in a more suburban area? Out of 89 students, 14 mentioned the author; not to ask questions, but to gather information needed to make sense of the text. For example, when talking about the poem "Nikki Rosa," students made a variety of statements about the author of/voice in the poem: "She sounds angry at White people"; "She's Black, but Giovanni is not a name you hear in a lot of Blacks. It sounds Italian"; "She wrote the poem when she was more successful." One looked at the juxtaposition of "Christ" and "masses" and said that the author was a very moral person and that this was a very moral poem.

Some students offered the prior information that had been used to make sense of the poem. This was generally the case when students had read enough literature from a particular background to have some sense of the culture represented. More specifically, this was the case for "Nikki Rosa," the African American poem. One student said that the poem was about slavery days because it mentions no inside toilet. (Similarly, one student thought that the Chinese story was American because "the father got rich off of slave labor.") One student simply said, "Blacks have strong ties." Four students touched on the racial tension embedded in "Nikki Rosa" to some degree. One said, "We always feel we're superior to [African Americans] . . . we have always put [them] down." Another student also noted the presence of prejudice in our society. One student said that when European American people write about African American people, "They just go back to your childhood and say how rough it was for you to grow up." Only one student (from Tanzania) went beyond the immediacy of the poem to extrapolate, "It explains that [when others] aren't of the same race as you are, they usually just don't understand about your life, like if they try to write a book or a movie about you, you couldn't have the same interpretation as a person of your own race would."

A few students provided some cultural information about the background of the texts. One student simply said, "[The author] might have been an Indian" but could not explain why she thought this. Another said that the vocabulary used in "Nikki Rosa" was a female vocabulary; this same student recognized the Native American origins of "Grandmother Spider" because of the names. Another, also talking about "Grandmother Spider," said, "I know they're into nature."

For the other cultures represented in the texts, results are more individualized. For some students, having no background knowledge of a culture really impeded their understanding of a text. Two who read the Native American story needed a great deal of information in order to make any sense of the text. Both said that they did not understand at all, and neither could begin to articulate just what was needed in order for the story to make sense. (This style of this story echoes certain oral traditions, which means that it lacks the straightforward chronology that many readers expect from stories.) One student asked about the position of rats in Chinese folklore. She wanted to know if the rat in Lawrence Yep's story was culturally symbolic or if its appearance was just in the story. (This question could be seen as a request not for information, but for guidance to how to talk about a story, because classroom talk about literature is often very different from everyday discussion about, say, the plot of a movie.)

If the students were asked to frame the selection in a cultural context, they did provide some information. When the interview began with the question, "This is a story from X culture. What do you expect it to contain?" many could provide some information. An interesting example is the student who, when questioned about Hispanic literature, replied that she expected Mexican (not Hispanic) literature to contain strong family ties and many religious allusions. After reading the story (which was not Mexican, although it was Hispanic), she said that the story was not Mexican because it did not have these elements. Several students said that Native Americans have legends, and one said that although the Chinese story could have been American in theme (e.g., that "the world is too crazed with money"), she knew that the painting of bad luck symbols was distinctly Chinese. Americans, she said, would have messed with the plumbing.

We see that students can make sense of a text by discussing the story in classroom language, which generally means a discussion about author intent, genre, or literary device (such as theme or moral). When cultural issues were raised, they were couched in these terms.

If the students did not raise cultural issues overtly as matters of knowledge and as a basis for interpretation, some of them did so in other ways. There were students who rejected the text as alien because of the experiences it described, as did the student who said, "I'm not Black and I've never lived with 'no inside toilet.'" But there were also students who rejected a text because the text itself was alien, as did one student who disliked "Grandmother Spider," who found no way to read it with any understanding, but who denied that this lack of understanding was because of a lack of background information about Native American beliefs and methods of storytelling. Instead, the story was "boring." The difference between these two responses is that the first recognizes cultural or experiential differences, whereas the other, in having no access to the text itself, does not.

A good number of students rejected texts for various reasons. A number of White students rejected "Nikki Rosa" because they themselves were not African American or did not share the background of the author/voice of the poem. For example, three students rejected the poem because (they thought) it implied that only an African American person can have an unhappy childhood, and one student rejected it because she wasn't poor and did not have an "alcoholic father." Of the 13 who originally rejected the poem, two reread the poem and found it positive, which changed their original objection. One student disliked the Honduran story "The Proof" because she thought it was about a rich family, and she did not like the mother who "doesn't really do anything, she just stays home." Two students did not like or understand Chato, the Mexican American, urban protagonist of one story.

Students also rejected the unfamiliar. Some rejected "Nikki Rosa" because of a dislike of poetry, or were turned off by certain words or titles, such as the title "Grandmother Spider." One did not like the Chinese story because it wasn't possible; she called it "really weird."

Stereotyping

In addition to rejecting the text as a whole, a number of students mentioned or referred to stereotypes. Some of the stereotypes were rather neutral, as in the comment, "Indian legends always have lots of symbolism" or that the "magic and mystery" of one story were typically Chinese. One said that an Hispanic story took place in the United States because there was mention of eye shadow and makeup in the story. One student, when reading the Chinese story, commented that the poor treatment of the workers reminded him of how slaves were treated here in the United States. Most of the responses concerned the stereotypes of African Americans available to us in American society: poor, hard-working, church-going, and jazz-playing. Three students did not use these stereotypes in reacting to the poem, but mentioned that the "poor black" is a stereotype. Three students focused on the stereotypes of poverty, without bringing up the racial element of the poem. For these students, poverty was ugly regardless of location or race.

Two students were surprised by the "normalcy" of the suburban setting in one of the Hispanic texts, and another student implied that people with Hispanic names could not be American. Four students focused on a line that read "your father's drinking" in "Nikki Rosa," immediately translating this into alcoholism. One of these students also thought that the word *stock* referred to drugs, and that the father was a drug dealer.

Most of the stereotyping occurred in response to the African American text, perhaps because the students are more familiar with or more conscious of the stereotypes concerning that group than the other groups. In other cases, it formed the basis of what I. A. Richards (1928) called a "stock response," and at worst could lead to an interpretation of the text that was questionable. An example of this would be students' reaction to the poem "Nikki Rosa." Because much African American literature taught in schools focuses on the experience of the African American in a racist society, students come to expect anger and poverty in any African American poem, and encounter difficulties when the text is less straightforward. Or students, through the media or through experience, come to understand that "Hispanic" is another word for Mexican migrant worker or Puerto Rican, and all "Hispanics" get lumped under that category. The same thing happens with words like *alcohol*—everyone who drinks is an alcoholic.

What this tells us is that students are limited in the information they receive about others. And before we blame the media, or poor reading lists, or student apathy, let us just say that this lack of exposure could simply be because students are young.

Interpreting.   One phenomenon of the interpretation of literature that has long been noted by scholars is the tendency for readers to invest themselves into the work and seek to make the text more pleasant than it is. It is a form of stock response that has been called "happiness binding" (Squire, 1963). Thirty-six students gave responses of this sort, 24 of them involving the poem "Nikki Rosa." Eight students said that it was about African American love, and 16 did not mention the negative features mentioned in the poem but said they thought the point was that "even though she was poor, she was happy." Four students saw "Grandmother Spider" as a tale about overcoming obstacles, and three thought that the point of "You Are Now Entering the Human Heart" was that the teacher finally overcame her fear of snakes. Although these "happiness binding" answers are sometimes plausible, they also serve to ignore certain elements of the texts. For example, the teacher in "Human Heart" does not overcome her fear of snakes—her sense of control and of power are destroyed by the episode with the snake. This "happiness binding" is promoted by literature instruction in schools, because many of the teachers participating in this study approach the teaching of literature through the use of themes, an approach that is supported by literature textbooks. And the stories in reading textbooks often have happy endings, or the received interpretation is optimistic rather than gloomy.

Obviously, those students who looked for pleasant interpretations showed a certain amount of misunderstanding, although not always on a cultural level. The misunderstandings can be broadly generalized into the following categories:

- A lack of awareness of cultural institutions, such as the strength of the Roman Catholic Church in the everyday life of many Hispanic cultures, the role of the male, or the structure of the household.
- A lack of information about beliefs. An example of the first is the student who dropped the "Spider" from "Grandmother Spider" because she did not know about Native American relationships with animals.
- A lack of awareness of alternative literary norms, as the example of the student who said that the Native American story needed "A beginning, a middle, and an end, not a middle, a beginning, and an end."
- A lack of awareness of a culture's literary heritage. For many, this appeared in the ignorance about African American literature beyond *Black Boy* and *Raisin in the Sun*. One student dismissed "Nikki Rosa" with an implication that African Americans only write about being unhappy.
- A lack of awareness of social phenomena, such as the prevalence of poverty in the United States.
- A lack of awareness of the author or narrator. This appeared in the "assumption of a male voice." The assumption of voice is fine, but it begs the question, "Would we read something differently if we knew it was a woman's voice?" Would more students have noted the snake attendant's careless dismissal of the teacher's terror if they had seen the observer as a female?

Another aspect of interpretation is that although students did differentiate between the pairs of texts they read, most did not differentiate the texts on a cultural level. One student, in comparing stories, said, "Both have something to do with cultures. They're different because the story tells you that they're trying to get something. The poem seems to tell you that the person is unhappy." A second student also tried to compare cultures and ended up comparing the "fantasy" of one text with the "reality" of the poem. Another, in response to a request to compare, replied, "They both had their difficulties, but they came from different backgrounds. I don't think her mother [in "Nikki Rosa"] is really worried about makeup or getting dressed up but hers [from "It Happened that Day"] is." This is a comparison based more on economics than on culture (although different economic situations do produce different cultural situations).

What all this really means is that students do not have the vocabulary or experience to talk about the culture of a text or in a text. They can talk about genre, theme, and characterization, because this is how they are taught to talk about a text. They cannot compare different cultures without more information and practice. And they cannot leave the culture of the classroom as their vantage point.

Judging.   Because the students were asked to rate the texts they read, and most seemed eager to talk about their personal reactions, there were a number of responses that dealt with judgment. Some of the judgments dealt with style, and some with content, but most dealt with personal impact and identification. The stylistic criteria included liking the story because of a neat ending, because of the language used, or because it was familiar and therefore accessible. Students disliked a text because it was "boring and had no meaning," "boring and dragged on and on," "confusing," or "too realistic and depressing." A few students mentioned the ending, the wording or the symbolism, or the impossibility of the story.

Their reasons for liking the content of a text varied. Many liked "Nikki Rosa" because "it had a point" and "told the truth." Two mentioned liking a text because of the fear that a certain character felt. Two disliked poems in general, and two disliked characters in the story enough to dislike the entire text. One student said that he liked a text because it was modern and about an everyday kid, which he liked. Another liked a story because "It gave me a picture as I was reading it."

Many of the judgments dealt with the impact of the story and the students' ability to identify with the characters, the culture, or the situation. There were two who could relate to the story and who therefore liked it: "I like Indian culture" and "She's Black like me." Two identified with the poem because they themselves were African American, two responded to the text because of their own childhood memories, one identified with the teacher of "Human Heart" because she herself was scared of snakes, and one identified with a statement that indicated that women often change their looks, eyes, and makeup. One student identified with the Chinese story, saying, "I know people who get rich and feel superior." There was one identification with a text because of childhood memories and race. Two students identified with young Chato de Shamrock because of his need for his friends, and one young White male identified with "Nikki Rosa" because his own father was in prison (although the father in the poem is not in prison) and his family was struggling to stay together. One identified with "Nikki Rosa" because it was about a girl trying to be strong.

It seems clear that identification is an important contributor to both understanding and judgment, although the identification may at times be a form of projection into the text rather than introjection of the text into the reader's world.

From the results of the pilot study, then, students appear to respond to literature on a personal basis. Even when told that a text is from another culture, students do not look at the text as a cultural artifact. Instead, they read it according to how they are taught to read literature by first reacting to the story or to the characters therein. They tend to ignore the author and the location of the text in their stated responses.

By high school, most students can read a text and are adept at filling in the "missing information" gaps. When they have problems understanding what they read, these are seen as problems with the writer or with themselves as readers, not as problems in their cultural knowledge. Because students do not perceive cultural differences, they change neither their criteria for judging what they read nor their discourse concerning texts. Nor do they experience pleasure or displeasure according to the culture aspect of the text. When a text is from a different culture, they seek to accommodate it to their own view of the world. And, because we were interviewing students in a school setting, we found that most students read texts and responded as if for a teacher.

Students disliked texts that were "boring," and these were generally texts that they did not understand. Lack of comprehension generally meant that the initial reaction would be one of dislike. But many students, after discussing the text with the interviewer, changed their opinion about the text. When students were given enough information about a text (so that the text made sense) they liked it.

The question then becomes, how can teachers make texts more accessible to students and therefore more acceptable to them? Teachers themselves are often at a loss to supply specifics about a culture, so they teach thematically. Because teachers may not have a great deal of knowledge about other cultures, students may not see that lack of information about the text's background culture can be a problem. Instead, students rely on their own knowledge (including misinformation) to understand a text. Making an effort not to explain a culture appears to have its dangers, in that students will perpetuate their own myths and misconceptions about "others" and one point of multicultural education—that of learning about other viewpoints—is lost. The interviews with students suggest that unless some attempt is made to give students some factual information about the background culture of texts, then the cycle of one voice, rejection of unknown voices, could continue.

The problem with making multicultural texts accessible is twofold. In many different writings, Alan Purves pointed out that teachers teach from a canon, whether or not they recognize this fact, and may be prejudiced against works from outside of the canon. Their position with respect to texts results in part from the way they have been taught to view texts and their interpretation of them. For example, the students who assumed a male voice for the female story show that many students are still being taught that the dominant voice in our society is still White European male. One may well wonder how easily a new reading list (or canon) can be implemented, one that is a natural counterpoint to the standard voice—with both female and minority authors and protagonists. Before education can be multicultural, there must first be recognition that a dominant voice persists and that literature is generally taught in that voice.

The second problem is that teachers also find it difficult to approach "other" texts with new eyes. Students are taught to read texts within the framework of his or her literature teacher, and have trouble reading a text for themselves or for itself.

On the basis of this preliminary study, it is clear that a more focused set of interviews is needed to explore precisely what sorts of information and guidance students and teachers might need. Of particular importance is the degree to which the personalizing of the response and the desire for identification with the text hampers students' ability to read texts from other cultures. Also important is the influence of happiness binding in their reading of texts from cultures other than their own. Of greatest importance is the suggestion raised in the interviews that because students tend to read texts out of their own experience, they have trouble reading texts from cultures other than their own. They appear to have little knowledge of other cultures and little practice in reading literature as the expression of a culture and an author who is influenced by his or her culture. Because this preliminary study suggests that students have limited knowledge of other cultures, it is important to view this and other tentative conclusions from a broader perspective.

THE NATIONAL SURVEY OF STUDENT RESPONSES
TO MULTICULTURAL LITERATURE

The intent behind the second part of the research was to see if a larger sample yielded significant patterns in the ways that students respond to or view particular pieces of literature from other cultures. The data collection consisted of a national survey in which students were asked to read several texts and respond to some questions.

Because we wanted to make sure that our sample had relatively large percentages of various ethnic groups, we contacted the National Center for Educational Statistics (NCES) in order to draw a sample of schools. In particular, we wanted to make sure to have a significant number of Native American students and Asian students. From NCES we received a national sample of 60 schools in which there was a large proportion of students from these groups as well as Hispanic Latino and African American. We then contacted the schools suggested, asking them to provide willing teachers of classes in which the majority of students were in the target ages of between 13 and 17 years.

Meanwhile we selected texts that were short, complete (no excerpts), and had certain cultural indications. (By "cultural indications" we mean words in another language, or reference to an experience significant to a particular group, or any other indications in the text that this piece of literature "belonged" to a particular culture.) We found 18 texts that we decided to use, and after receiving permission from the schools to conduct our research, we then sent our survey packets.

There were two kinds of packets. The first kind, which provided the main data for this study, consisted of three texts, spiraled so that each packet contain a folktale, a piece by a male and a piece by a female, and with no two texts from the same culture in the same packet. Each packet also contained forced-choice questions about each of these texts. The questions were drawn from previous studies that had looked at response to literature across cultures (e.g., Purves, 1973). The first asked students to select from a list of questions that might be asked about a literary work those that the student considered most important. The second asked the student to rate the selection or a character in the selection according to a set of multidimensional scales, like the semantic differential. Both proved to be good indicators of the response style of individuals and groups. (Please see the Appendix for a list and description of each text.)

The other packet was the written form. Students were asked to read two (as opposed to three) texts, and to respond to questions. They were also encouraged to write on the texts and to draw pictures. We coded these responses, but so much of the data were blank, and the number of responses was so small ($n = 61$), that we did not run any analysis on the responses. Instead, these responses were examined for salient or enlightening comments or insights.

These texts were distributed to the schools, students responded to them as in a test situation, and the surveys were returned to us. We did not have a good rate of return. Out of 60 schools contacted, 10 replied. We had hoped to collect data from close to 1,000 students; instead, we collected surveys from just over 500, and of this number, only 437 were complete.

The statistical analyses were done on 16 of the 18 texts. Two texts had to be dropped because of the small number of responses.

THE THREE MOST IMPORTANT QUESTIONS

This part of the analysis focuses on the three postreading questions that students chose as the most important regarding the text selection they read. The analysis, done by Shouming Li, was done in two ways.

Ethnicity-Based Analysis

The ethnicity-based analysis is meant to answer the research question of whether a certain cultural group chose a particular question as the most important. This is done by a cross-tabulation that shows the percentage of students in each cultural group who selected each of the 14 questions. Because each student read three individual texts in each session, an average percentage was computed across the texts.

Two cross-tabulations were made. In the general analysis, the 14 questions were divided into two general types representing text comprehension and personal response, as shown in the following lists:

Type 1: *Text Comprehension Questions*
    What does this poem/story mean?
    What is this poem/story about?
    Where and when did this poem/story take place?
    What does this poem/story tell me about the author and his or her feelings and beliefs?
    What does this poem tell me about _____ culture and why they are the way they are?
    How is this poem/story representative of the _____ culture?
    How can we explain the way people behave in this poem/story?

Type 2: Personal Response Questions
What is my personal response to this poem/story?
Could this poem/story have taken place where I live?
What other stories does this remind me of?
Does the author use words and phrases differently from most writers I know?
Is this a proper subject for a poem/story?
Is this a good poem/story?
Does this poem/story teach any lesson about human life and society?

In a more detailed analysis, the same questions were further divided into four types: text comprehension, cultural understanding, personal response, and value judgment.

Type 1: Text Comprehension Questions
What does this poem/story mean?
What is this poem/story about?
Where and when did this poem/story take place?
What does this poem/story tell me about the author and his or her feelings and beliefs?

Type 2: Cultural Understanding Questions
What does this poem tell me about _____ culture and why they are the way they are?
How is this poem/story representative of the _____ culture?
How can we explain the way people behave in this poem/story?

Type 3: Personal Response Questions
What is my personal response to this poem/story?
Could this poem/story have taken place where I live?
What other stories does this remind me of?
Does the author use words and phrases differently from most writers I know?

Type 4: Value Judgment Questions
Is this a proper subject for a poem/story?
Is this a good poem/story?
Does this poem/story teach any lesson about human life and society?

Questions of First Importance

The majority of students from all cultural groups chose questions dealing with comprehension as the most important. As Tables 2.2 and 2.3 show, the percentage of students choosing comprehension questions is the highest in both general and detailed analysis.

Questions of Second Importance

For the second most important question, students still tended to choose comprehension questions, but the percentage of students choosing response questions also increased, especially for African Americans, Hispanic Americans, and Euro-

TABLE 2.2

Percentage of Students Choosing Comprehension Versus Response Questions as the Most Important (General Analysis)

	Comprehension	Response
African American	72.6	27.4
Native American	68	32
Hispanic American	77.9	22.1
Asian American	69.6	30.4
European American	72	28

TABLE 2.3

Percentage of Students Choosing Comprehension Versus Response Questions as the Most Important (Detailed Analysis)

	Comprehension		Reaction	
	Text	Culture	Response	Judgment
African American	56	16.6	16.3	11.1
Native American	2.5	15.4	18	14.1
Hispanic American	59	19	9.5	12.5
Asian American	49.3	20.2	14.5	16
European American	52.5	19.5	17.5	10.5

TABLE 2.4

Percentage of Students Choosing Comprehension Versus Response Questions as the Second Most Important (General Analysis)

	Comprehension	Response
African American	59.1	40.9
Native American	64	36
Hispanic American	58.3	41.7
Asian American	62.3	37.7
European American	57.1	42.9

pean Americans. As Table 2.4 indicates, close to half of the students in these cultural groups selected response questions as the second most important.

A detailed analysis (Table 2.5) further shows that although text comprehension still has the largest percentage of students among all categories, its absolute percentage actually decreased from Table 2.4, and the decrease was rather dramatic for African Americans, Native Americans, and Hispanic Americans. Meanwhile, there is an overall increase in the percentage of students choosing the rest three categories of questions. In fact, the differences in percentage among them appear much narrowed from Table 2.4, although the category of cultural understanding still remains the highest percentage among the three.

Questions of Third Importance

General analysis (Table 2.6) reveals little change, from the same analysis of the second most important questions, in the distribution of students choosing comprehension versus response questions. Except for the Native American group, the pattern seems to have stabilized, with comprehension questions maintaining a marginal or weak majority. The Native Americans were the only cultural group that reversed the pattern of comprehension over response. As shown in Table 2.6, more students (56%) in that group selected response rather than comprehension questions as the third most important.

The detailed analysis (Table 2.7) further reveals that a rather large percentage of Native Americans (44%) selected value judgment questions as the third most important. Notice also that for Hispanic and Asian American, questions of cultural

TABLE 2.5

Percentage of Students Choosing Comprehension Versus Response Questions as the Second Most Important (Detailed Analysis)

	Comprehension		Reaction	
	Text	Culture	Response	Judgment
African American	34.3	24.8	19.8	21.1
Native American	32	32	17.3	18.7
Hispanic American	30.7	27.6	18.1	23.5
Asian American	39.1	23.2	23.2	14.5
European American	32.3	25	24.2	18.5

TABLE 2.6

Percentage of Students Choosing Comprehension Versus Response Questions as the Third Most Important (General Analysis)

	Comprehension	Response
African American	54.3	45.7
Native American	44	56
Hispanic American	60.6	39.4
Asian American	62.3	37.7
European American	54.5	45.5

TABLE 2.7

Percentage of Students Choosing Comprehension Versus Response Questions
as the Third Most Important (Detailed Analysis)

	Comprehension		Reaction	
	Text	Culture	Response	Judgment
African American	31.8	22.5	25.8	19.9
Native American	26.7	17.3	12	44
Hispanic American	28.5	32.1	19	20.4
Asian American	24.6	37.7	21.7	15.9
European American	27.5	26.9	21.7	23.9

understanding have the largest percentage of students (32.1% and 37.7%, respectively). Although African Americans and Native Americans show a larger percentage of selecting text comprehension questions, European Americans seem to be equally concerned with text comprehension and cultural understanding.

Text-Based Analysis.   The purpose of text-based analysis is to investigate whether students reading a selection of their own cultural background reacted differently from those reading about an outside culture. Again, the same cross-tabulations as in the ethnicity-based analysis were made, but the unit of analysis is each of the sixteen individual texts.

Because we had sixteen texts with five ethnic/cultural groups, we had a possibility of 80 sets of responses. Of these, 16 had to be discounted because of too few respondents in a group. We knew that the majority of patterns would start with comprehension, which indeed proved to be the case. Thirty-two of the response sets had comprehension questions rated as the first and second most important questions to be asked about a text; another 28 also had comprehension as the most important question. We are left with four sets of responses that indicate, for certain texts, comprehension was not the most important question to be asked.

One of these texts was "The People Could Fly," an African American folktale. Native American students rated questions of judgment as the most important question to be asked about this text, with questions of culture as the second and third most important questions to ask. One Native American student wrote that "The selection makes fun of a serious subject." European American students indicated that questions of culture, all the way across the board, were most important, as reflected in such comments as "Most slaves had faith" and "No matter how life was and how bad it was nothing could stop them from living." The other three groups followed the expected pattern of focusing on comprehension.

African American students felt that questions of culture were the first and second most important questions to ask about the Puerto Rican tale "Juan Bobo," and that judgment was the third most important question. Again, other groups followed expected patterns. The same group—African Americans—indicated that questions of judgment and then comprehension were of primary importance when reading

"The Rat in the Wall," a Chinese tale. We discuss the significance of these findings in the next section, when we take another look at culture–text interaction.

One-Way Analysis.   After figuring the descriptive statistics for students, and seeing if students interacted with texts of their own culture in significant ways, we turned our attention to how students of specific cultures interacted with a particular text, looking for insights into possible culture–text interactions. We wanted to see if students from different ethnic backgrounds responded to the culture of the texts differently. We did this by asking, "On the basis of reading this story, how would you rate the portrayal of the _____ culture?" We presented students with a 5-point scale, ranging from 1 (*low*) to 5 (*high*). Characteristics presented to the students were: strong, passive, immoral, forceful, upright, unpleasant, gentle, complex, natural, religious, rigid, and traditional. We then ran one-way analyses on student ratings of the culture represented by the text. (In other words, after reading a particular story, students were asked if they thought that the culture from which the text came was, for example, religious.)

The initial analysis showed no interaction, so we created a 3-point scale by combining either end of our scale. *Low* and *somewhat low* were combined, and *high* and *somewhat high* were also merged. The middle point on the 5-point scale was considered neutral. In this way we did find some culture–text interaction.

The results of the analyses are summarized in Table 2.8. Examining the results of the one-way analyses demands that we look at the specifics of the text and its specific cultural allusions. Such an approach does not permit us to make broad generalizations about how x culture interacts with the texts from y culture, but it does permit us to make tentative statements.

A problem with this sort of analysis is that no matter how knowledgeable the researcher is about other cultures, he or she ultimately must still rely on his or her own experiences in interpreting the data, a fact that lends itself to bias and misinterpretation. Another problem with looking for differences in cultural reactions is that statistics may not really prove anything. Even if the differences observed are not due to chance, they still might be the result of biases in sampling or text selection, and they may not be culturally significant. This means that interpretations of the data are tentative and subject to discussion.

Results of the One-Way   We began with a general look at what characteristics students disagreed on, hoping that this information would provide an overview of cultural perceptions. It appears that cultures differ in their perception of what is unpleasant, what is natural, and what it means to be religious.

What texts inspired students to rate the background culture as unpleasant? One was "The People Could Fly," an African American tale set in the times of slavery. The group called "other" (which was predominantly European American) did not find the culture of the text to be unpleasant (1.3 on a 3-point scale), whereas African American students, Native American students, and Asian American students all found the story unpleasant (scores of 2.23, 2.6, and 2.03, respectively). It could be that these latter groups focused on the enslavement aspect of the story, with the brutal overseer and his whip, whereas the other group saw the story as one with a happy ending, because some of the slaves learn to fly, to escape their situation.

TABLE 2.8

Traits That Received Significantly Different Ratings by Different Ethnic Groups

Text Name	Text Culture	Name of Characteristic	Groups and Means
"The People Could Fly"	African American	Complex Religious Unpleasant	Other (European) 2.00 [n = 20] African Americans 2.71 [14] African Americans 2.71 [14] Hispanic Americans 1.88 [16] Other (European): 1.3 [20] African Americans: 2.23 [13] Native Americans: 2.6 [5] Hispanic Americans: 2.026 [16]
"Juan Bobo"	Hispanic (Puerto Rico)	Unpleasant	Native Americans: 1.00 [5] Asian Americans: 2.8 [5] Other (European): 2.4 [35]
"Nikki Rosa"	African American	Passive Unpleasant	African Americans 2.36 [12] Hispanic Americans: 1.45 [20] Other (European) 1.5 [28] Asian Americans 1.33 [6] Native Americans 3.00 [3]
"Devil Woman"	Hispanic (Mexican?)	Religious	Other (European) 2.55 [33] African Americans 1.71 [14]
"The Rat in the Wall"	Asian (Folk)	Natural	Other (European) 1.97 [31] Hispanic Americans 1.37 [19]
		Traditional	Other (European) 2.5 [30] Hispanic Americans 1.95 [20]
"Grandmother Spider"	Native American	Natural	Other (European) 2.54 [28] African Americans 1.67 [12]
"Yellow Woman"	Asian American (Chinese)	Immoral Natural	Other (European) 1.46 [26] African Americans 2.3 [10] African Americans 2.91 [11] Other (European) 2.07 [26]
"Theme for English B"	African American	Upright	Asian Americans 1.67 [6] African Americans 2.58 [12] Other (European) 2.50 [28]
"From My Grandmother"	Native American	Strong Religious	Other (European) 2.79 [19] African Americans 2.13 [15] Hispanic Americans 2.12 [17] Hispanic Americans 1.59 [17] Other (European) 2.47 [19]

Sophia Mallett, an African American graduate student who reviewed the data for an independent study, offered this interpretation of the results:

"The People Could Fly" . . . evoked strong reactions from many African American students. Their reactions may stem from their comprehension of the historical background of the black experience throughout the malicious event of slavery. Toby, the old man in the story, is seen as a sort of guardian angel, the protector. It is interesting to note that most of the African American students didn't question why Toby in the conclusion of the story couldn't set the slaves free. The lack of this type of questioning perhaps [may] stem from their historical knowledge that during slavery gaining one's freedom was a great victory and many died in the process. . . . The event of slavery rarely produced happy endings.

Perhaps students were unclear as to which culture this text belonged. Although it was from a collection of African American folktales, students might have seen it not so much as a "real" African American text, but one that resulted from the European culture that created slavery. And perhaps another reason that European American students did not find the story unpleasant was because, as one student wrote, "To me it sounds like a story I've heard a million times before, just another person changing a few details, but still sounding like the same old story. Using wings to fly away is convenient." This weariness with "the same old story" is as dismissive as the statements mentioned earlier, statements such as "most slaves had faith." Other students, maybe less weary ones, became more involved with the story. A Portuguese American student focused on the slaves' attainment of freedom. An Hispanic girl wrote, "I didn't understand why Toby couldn't take the slaves that couldn't fly. . . . If the slaves could fly why didn't they fly away from being a slave?" An Asian American student, who read the story as fiction set in an imaginary world, wrote, "The people who could fly were treated differently and used as slaves. It's the same as the original Black slaves who were treated differently because of their skin." Sophia Mallett suggested that "Their misunderstanding of the metaphorical meaning of flying may result from their foreign relation in comprehending the historical background of Black culture and the profound effects that slavery had and still has on AfroAmericans."

The culture that produced "Juan Bobo," who is an Hispanic version of the literary and folk "fool" or "simpleton" common to many cultures, was also considered unpleasant by Asian and European American students (2.8 and 2.4), whereas Native American students did not find it unpleasant at all (1.00). In this story, Juan Bobo is simply a fool, as opposed to the more clever roles he plays in other tales. He disobeys his mother, which is perhaps why the Asian American students found it unpleasant. He also inadvertently kills his baby sibling. But the style of the text is upbeat, almost silly, and Hispanic students produced a mean of 2.00. One wrote, "The story should be changed because the boy tried his best and that's just as good as he gets. And his mom was very rude. Story of responsibility." Another wrote, "I like stories that can project everything that is happening in my mind. I could see everything he was doing upon reading it." A third Hispanic student commented, "Something that was missing . . . is what happened to Juan after. Did he become a good, responsible boy?" Non-Hispanic students were much more outraged, and more inclined to find fault. A Portuguese American student wrote, "I think they (Juan Bobo and his mother) both need therapy! This story is ridiculous. Who wants to read about a sick little boy killing everything in sight? You see enough tragedies in real life." An Asian American wrote "[The story] is stupid because the kid Juan Bobo is so stupid it's not even funny. . . . I would of [killed him] if he killed my kid if I had one. Then I would chop him up and feed him to the animals. [This was in reference to the mother's reaction, which was to beat Juan Bobo 'until he was nearly dead.'] This kid is such a idiot. I really hate this story it made me mad." An "other," who was aghast that anyone would leave Juan Bobo alone with a baby, house, and livestock, wrote, "You could see he's mentally retarded. His mother sounds like a witch, very aggressive. She is very careless and doesn't think things over." Another Portuguese American student commented, "She must not of taught him very well."

The third text that had divided ratings for the characteristic "unpleasant" was the poem "Nikki Rosa." Asian American students did not find the culture particularly unpleasant (1.33), but Native American students did, giving the culture of the poem a 3.00. Still, a caveat is necessary, because only six Asian American and three Native American students read this text.

We are doubtful that students were actually rating the culture of the text. We see the prevalence of the "unpleasant" characteristic as a judgment on the content of the text and not as a judgment on the culture itself. But this observation does not invalidate the different perceptions that cultures may have of a particular story or poem, and the fact that African American students in particular refused to seek the "happiness binding" element of the first text. The same split occurs with the rating of the poem "Yellow Woman." African American students found this poem of Asian enslavement very immoral; European American students found it only slightly (if at all) immoral. Once again, we would hazard the opinion that this is a case of identification. African American students identify with the enslaved culture and condemn the dominant culture. Unfortunately, few students commented on this poem.

African American students were distinctive in their patterns of response. Of the nine texts that were marked as eliciting different ratings from different cultures, African American students' responses were significantly different in seven of these, and generally (quite generally) in juxtaposition with the European American students. Their responses to African American texts are significant; what is interesting, and maybe even important, is that no other culture responded to a text of its "own" culture in a significant way. In other words, Hispanic students, when reading an Hispanic text, did not find either the text or the culture particularly religious, unpleasant, or anything else.

However, African American students did find their "own" texts distinctive. We have already discussed the "unpleasant" rating of "The People Could Fly"; African American students also found this text very complex (with a mean of 2.71, vs. European American students' mean of 2.00) and very religious (again, with a mean of 2.71; Hispanic American students had a score of 1.88).

For the poem "Nikki Rosa," a poem about how one's [Black] childhood is rewritten by White biographers, African American students did not touch on whether or not the text was "unpleasant" but they did find it very passive. They rated it with a 2.36, whereas Hispanic American and European American students did not find it passive (1.45 and 1.50, respectively).

The other African American text, "Theme for English B," was also rated very upright by African and European American students. Asian American students did not see the culture of this text as upright, perhaps because the text shows what could be seen as a disrespect for the teacher. Then again, perhaps students were confused. An Asian (Cambodian) student wrote, "Well I think this person is trying to say that a White man would want to be a Black person but a Black person won't want to [be] a White person either"; "This selection is trying to say no matter if you're White, Mexican, Afro-American, Chinese or any other race we are the same in the inside and out and we act the same even if sometimes we hate the other. Rating of 3 [midpoint on a 5-point scale of how much the student liked the text] because he likes violence." Actually, there is no mention of violence in the poem, and the tone is somewhat challenging as a young man asserts that being African American is not like being White.

What does the fact that African American students strongly respond to their own texts tell us? Are their responses part of a cultural inheritance, or are they the product of a school system that promotes the history of the African American as erstwhile slave, current underdog? African Americans seemed to respond differentially; they saw "The People Could Fly" as religious, and seemed to focus on the horrors of slavery. They saw the poem "Nikki Rosa" as passive because the narrator (a child) is content with her life; she does not seem to challenge the status quo the way that the narrator of "Theme for English B" does.

The concept of what is religious according to different cultures was also evident in the way different student groups rated various texts. We have mentioned that "The People Could Fly" was considered very religious by African American students but not religious by Hispanic American students; the text "The Devil Woman," a Mexican tale in which a young man meets the devil, who is disguised as a woman, was not considered religious by African American students, but European American students found this text quite religious. (Hispanic students scored right in the middle of the 5 means.) We don't know if this difference is due to one in the definition of religion or to a judgment of the texts. An African American student wrote, "The importance of the story is the strong belief Mexicans have in superstition and religion"; perhaps, then, superstition and the beliefs of "superstitious people" do not constitute religion.

The written comments to this story point to a gender difference, something not evident in the analysis. A few female students (mostly "others") requested more information about the fiancée. One wrote, "I would like to know why Manuel's sweetheart broke off the wedding!" Another: "I don't understand why his fiancée called off their wedding just because he almost died. You would think she would love him more and want to stand by him." There were also comments along more feminist lines: "Manuel should have listened to his soon-to-be wife. It proves that men should trust women." A female Hispanic student wrote, "Ticks me off when the author says, 'If anyone does not believe in these things, then let him look at the scars on my back.' I hate it when they say him or he (male gender) when they are describing people as a whole. They should say them instead."

The Hispanic American population was neutral in rating the religious aspect of "Devil Woman," producing that the mean was almost exactly a 2. It did score "From My Grandmother," a Native American poem, as not very religious, which contrasts with the European American rating of very religious. This means that the scores of European American students have twice been significantly different in the area of religion, higher than the other groups. We have no explanation for this result. Perhaps European Americans are more willing to call spiritual or supernatural elements religious, whereas for other cultures this word might imply organized religion.

Although European, African, and Hispanic American students saw the culture of "From My Grandmother" as strong, European American students rated this culture as strong significantly more than the other two groups.

Three texts received scores of "natural." One of these was "How Grandmother Spider Brought the Light," a Native American creation tale of the gift of fire. In this story, animals are both people and animals. European American students found this story quite natural, but Hispanic Americans found it very unnatural, and the scores of African Americans are very close to those of this latter group. It appears that students read "unnatural" as "unreal," although perhaps students' familiarity with the structure of the text (i.e., the appearance of a theme or moral) makes a text appear "natural." For example, in response to "Grandmother Spider" one student wrote, "I liked it. It proves you don't have to be strong to do something." African American students also rated the culture of "The Rat in the Wall" as very unnatural, although European American students rated it as only slightly unnatural. European American students also saw the culture of this text as very traditional. Hispanic American students did not see this culture as traditional.

The story is about a young Chinese boy whose family moves into a cursed house, a house with a giant rat. In a way, the text is more accessible than some of the others that we chose, because is a story written in linear chronology ("Grandmother Spider" was written in a more circular fashion, holding true to oral traditions), and could be construed as a moral tale (which it is) or a scary story, a genre that is familiar to many students. It is interesting that Hispanic American students saw this text as neither natural nor traditional (one wrote, "The story shouldn't be changed because it talks about Native Americans"), whereas European American students saw it as both.

Interestingly, when Hispanic American students scored significantly differently than other groups, their scores were always at the low end of the scales, with the exception of the rating of "unpleasant" for "The People Could Fly," but even here they were lower than the other groups. Still, there is no pattern to what texts or what characteristics warranted low marks, except that they never scored significantly on Hispanic texts.

The other text that was rated as natural was "Yellow Woman," which was rated as very natural by African American students (who had also rated it as immoral) and only slightly natural by European American students (who had rated it low on the immoral scale).

Discussion About the Two Studies

We don't see a general trend in terms of cultural responses to cultural texts. Students tend to interact with individual stories, seeing stories as things that have meaning and are good or bad. From the results of the cross-tabulation analysis, we know that students perceive the initial critical questions as the same for all stories; all stories are therefore to be approached initially in the same way, regardless of culture. But after comprehension had been addressed, questions about culture become more important as the second and third questions.

The preliminary study called for greater numbers, which this study certainly provided. We can now see that the patterns of response outlined by the first study are not just the styles of individual students. In particular, the pattern of needing to identify with the text in order to comprehend it is still evident. This need to identify—to find commonalties—serves to promote the use of thematic teaching, an approach that makes the teaching and learning of literature a little easier for both teachers and students, because background information to the text can remain minimal.

However, identification is more complex than originally thought. For example, students in the first study who identified with "Nikki Rosa" often said they did "because she's Black like me." Certainly, race can be something with which to identify, but the African American students from the second study who indicated an identification with "Yellow Woman" probably identified with the enslavement endured by the narrator, which means that a common history was the connection.

This identification with a different, but similar, history brings up a pattern that is becoming more and more evident in society at large. African American students perceived their "own" literature differently than other students did. The earlier study, which contained interviews with teachers, made mention of an attitude that a White teacher cannot teach African American literature. If there really is a strong sense of "ours" that cannot be shared, then one wonders what the purpose of teaching literature is.

Of course, this attitude could be the result of reading lists of African American texts that focus on the struggle of being African American in a White society. This experience, and the literature about this experience, although significant, are not the only paths to an understanding of "the Black Atlantic world" (Gilroy, 1992), and to limit this world to just this viewpoint, as reading lists have wont to do, is unfair to the inhabitants of this world, both White and Black.

The 1993 study did not fully answer the question of what problems seem endemic to the understanding of readers. Perhaps no study will be able to fully answer that question, but most, if not all, will point to the area of comprehension. The data in this study suggest that issues of culture, both in the reader and the text, will interact with the reading, influencing, and, if not comprehension, then certainly judgment.

A LOOK AT THE TWO STUDIES: WHAT WE KNOW NOW

What Students Learn From Multicultural Literature

From the other chapters in this book, it should become clear to the reader that the school is a culture unto itself. From the beginning of their school careers, students are carefully taught appropriate ways to respond to, and questions to ask about, a text. Students learn that some discussion topics are taboo, especially those concerning drugs and sex. And, because the teaching of literature is therapeutic (in that students are encouraged to identify with a protagonist or to learn some sort of moral lesson from the text), there can be little tolerance for moral ambiguity. (This is why, perhaps, we see so much "happiness binding" in literature discussion.) Because our investigations into the nature of student response to literature took place in this classroom culture, the responses we received were, for the most part, shaped by the culture of school.

We will see that teachers have a variety of reasons for including multicultural literature in their classes. Students have, for the most part, one reason for reading a nonmainstream text: It's required. Students are concerned with simply understanding a text, and thus cultural insight is far down on their list of priorities. In fact, students do not generally see a text as representing a culture, nor do they see themselves as representing any particular culture. Thus, for students, *multicultural literature* is a fancy term for reading. It's a test to see if they've learned to read the "right" way.

However, such a sweeping generalization isn't going to help teachers of literature in their classrooms. For one thing, students do bring some cultural baggage with them to a text, the weight of which influences how they understand a text. Hence, let us spend some time reviewing what we know about how students read a text in English class.

What Do We Know? We Know That Students Read to Understand

Teachers know this. As soon as the book is closed, students begin to compare notes on what happened. Often they will preface their search for understanding with a comment to the effect of, "I didn't like it. It was too hard," which means that students may lack enough information to make sense of a text. If the text is read for a book report, often the report consists of a simple retelling of the plot, so that students can show the teacher that they "got" the story.

We Also Know That Students Look for Connections

Connecting to a text—finding a common experience, liking a character, identifying with a character's feelings—is sometimes a key to understanding the text. The connections are often on a personal level, which is why reader response as a reading tool has been gaining in popularity in high school classrooms, although text-based analysis still dominates teaching. Teachers understand that students have to make connections to a text before they can understand it, and thus much literary response is centered around such topics as "What did you like in this story? Did you identify with anyone?"

Thus teachers often approach the literature thematically, emphasizing the universals in various texts and playing down cultural differences. This approach permits students to make initial connections with a text via the theme, but it does not guarantee that students will really understand a text. Because a story is written from the perspective, or within the parameters, of a culture (and quite possibly from a completely foreign point of view), students may need some culturally specific information to really understand a text. We have found that unless this information is given, students are often at a complete loss in making sense of a story. Yes, they may understand what happens in a story, but not why, and thus they may judge a test rather harshly. When students have some background in a culture, they can then read a story from that culture and respond in a more than typical fashion. That is, after their initial "I liked it," or "I didn't like it," they should be able to supply reasons for their like/dislike.

Students are given some conflicting messages about how to read. Because current literary theory now runs along reader response lines, many teachers try to teach the text as an isolated object, something that has no connections or meaning until the student makes some. Reader response encourages students to view the text as an artifact detached from a context and to be read in terms of personal response.

Students appear to have little knowledge of other cultures and little practice in reading literature as the expression of a culture and an author who is influenced by his or her culture. Multicultural literature attaches strings to a text, and it's clear that, for unfamiliar texts, students need to hold on to those strings. In other words, students need an author or more information to place the author in a context in order to really understand a text—only then can real connections be made.

We Know That Students Respond According to How They Are Taught, and We Know That Thematic Teaching Influences How Students Read

As Meléndez points out in chapter 5 of this volume, one definition of culture is an observable pattern of behaviors, attitudes, and beliefs—in other words, culture is a collection of habits. Students learn particular reading habits in school, habits that may or may not be conducive to studying the "otherness" of multicultural literature. Students very quickly learn how to use the language of the classroom, using words like *theme* and *plot* when discussing a story. Students learn to use these words even when they are unsure as to what the words really mean. They learn these words because such words figure greatly in classroom discussions about literature. When students are asked to explain why they like or dislike a story, they will most often cite reasons of personal impact and identification. However, they cannot as easily cite reasons as to why they dislike a text; in such a situation they usually dismiss the story as "boring."

Looking for connections can lead to a "stock response," which, in many classrooms, means trying to find a theme that can be applied to a story. This can sometimes lead to a questionable interpretation of the text. One particular stock response is to find a moral theme or lesson, such as, "Even though she was poor, she was happy." This "happiness binding" is also a tendency to make the text happier than it is.

Thus, thematic teaching and literature anthologies serve to teach students to read for the universals and to seek out happy endings if possible. We have already seen that students perceive the critical questions to be asked of a text to be the same for all texts, which means that, generally, texts are to be approached in the same way. Hence, when they have problems understanding what they read, they see these as problems with the writer or with themselves as readers, not as a lack of background knowledge to the text.

We Know That Classifying Students According to Ethnic Background Is a Problem

As teachers, we are always trying to balance between treating all students fairly and equally, and sensing differences in students that require slightly different approaches to teaching and classroom management. The compilers of literature anthologies also have this problem of trying to be fair to all students, in terms of representing all groups, making sure that no particular group is maligned in a story, and writing questions about a text that recognize different personal student responses as well as possible approaches a teacher might take with a particular text. All of us involved in education are aware that there is no one size that fits all in terms of stories to teach and teaching styles to assume. After all, if there were an across-the-board perfect fit in literature, reader response and multicultural education would be moot points.

We Know That Students Are Individuals, and Groups Are Made Up of Individual Students

There are as many types of readers as there are texts to read, which means that students will judge a text from a variety of reader stances. Students will like or dislike a text depending on how much action there is, how much they know of the background culture, and whether they simply understand the piece. These are merely personal preferences. Sometimes these preferences are a matter of classroom reading experiences. For example, some students may accept or reject a text on the basis of an author's background. Most notably this happens with African American texts, when students think that they will be reading one more "White guys are the oppressors" story; African American students, knowing that the author of a text is also African American, will generally feel that it is "theirs," regardless of subject.

We Know That Cultural Groups Vary in Responses

A bigger problem in teaching is the interaction of the student's culture and background with the material being studied. This is not the same as being sensitive to students' backgrounds; it means really knowing how one type of student will react with a particular representative text. For example, African American students were often significantly different from European American students in their patterns of response to texts, whereas no other culture responded to a text of its "own" culture in a significant way. In other words, Hispanic students, when reading an Hispanic text, did not find either the text or the culture particularly religious, unpleasant, or anything else. But in stories about oppression of a particular group, African American students tended to identify with the enslaved culture and condemn the dominant culture, whereas European American students remained neutral in their views of the cultures in the texts.

We Know That Members of Cultural Groups Vary According to Nationality or Other Background Factors

We have all, at some point in our lives, had to check a little box that labeled our cultural background. For many, this selection has been problematic. In the same way, choosing an Hispanic (or mainstream, or Asian) text is problematic, because no one text can ever be representative of an entire group. For example, in California, 59% of the school-age population is Hispanic. Some are Mexican Americans, some are "Chicanos," others are from Central America or South America, and still others are from Spain. And many of these students are also of European and Native American heritage as well. This means that an Hispanic student, upon being told that a text is Hispanic, may find little to identify with in the text. The next chapter in this volume takes up this issue in greater detail.

We Know That Multicultural Literature Demands a New Set of Reading Skills

In order to explain this statement, let us review what we know:

1. Students read to understand a text. If they do not understand the text, then either they are bad readers or the writer is a bad writer.
2. Students think they need to like a text in order to understand it.
3. Texts are not seen as representing a particular culture. Rather, texts represent universals.
4. There is no easy way to classify any one student according to larger groups.

So how do these items lead us to the belief that we need a new set of reading skills? Or rather, what are these new reading skills? Quite simply, students need to learn to read for differences. Teaching thematically, which means looking for the similarities, does not teach the critical thought that we want students to exhibit. Instead of being able to identify gaps in knowledge (and thereby possibly seeking new information), students simply reject a text that is unfamiliar. As teachers, we aren't posing problems to students with their reading; we're not giving students two opposing ideas and saying, "If you hold these two in your head you have two opposite thoughts. How do you reconcile them?" Instead, we say, "All ideas fall under one category or another. And here is the category." There are no problems to be considered with this approach, just easy answers. Thematic grouping tends to treat a work of literature superficially, and, at the end, it's hard to get students to abandon preconceptions.

We can get students to explore their own culture by exploring others. We can do this by teaching two books at once, and teaching students to read for differences, for possible misunderstandings. The changes in reading skills will not come overnight, because we, as teachers, need to change our own habits. This takes time.

3

A Case Study of The Responses of Caribbean Students to Multicultural Literature

❧ ◆ ❧

Gladys Cruz and José Meléndez

Looking at students in a large survey, using questionnaires and even written self-reports, paints but a rough picture of a generality of students. One needs to take a more microscopic view in order to see what details emerge that would illuminate the corners of the broad description.

To that end, this study examined the interplay of culture of the reader and that of the text within a reading situation shaped by the research procedures employed: that is, private readings followed by a one-to-one interview. The definitional approaches proposed by Williams (1961) are used in this discussion: *the ideal, the documentary,* and *the social.* The use of these constructs focuses on the lived cultural experiences:

As portrayed in the texts.
Of the readers as cultural beings.
Of the readers reading the text (the readers' transactions, responses, and interpretations).

Our attention was drawn toward the wide variety of responses given by the students catalogued under the rubric "Hispanic-Latino." We selected a small number of students from Dominican and the Puerto Rican groups (which were classified as "Hispanic-Latino" in the larger study) who were in an intensive summer program for students entering college. These we decided to interview in detail.

We examined and compared some of the cultural manifestations of precollege students from these two groups, particularly as such manifestations bear on the students' responses to literary texts from diverse cultures. We attempted to do this not under the umbrella of an ethnic or national conceptualization of culture, but by using Williams' (1961) theoretical contructs: the ideal, the documentary, and the social. The *ideal* refers to the absolute and universal values that can be seen to compose a timeless order. The *documentary* consists of the body of intellectual and imaginative work that records in detail human thought and experience. The *social* offers a description of a particular way of life that expresses certain meanings and values, not only in art and learning, but also in institutions and behavior.

An interview questionnaire geared toward extracting cultural knowledge and awareness from the students was prepared. The questionnaire was then tested with three students from each group in order to validate it. Next, the questionnaire was administered in interview form to 23 students. The taped interviews were transcribed, analyzed, and interpreted in order to answer the following research questions:

1. To what extent do the participants demonstrate:
   Knowledge of the concept of culture?
   An awareness of culture as lived experiences?

2. How do they demonstrate this knowledge and awareness in their responses to the literary texts encountered?

3. Do the two groups of participants differ according to the responses given to the diverse texts?

4. To what extent is the culture of the literary text acknowledged and/or manifested in the responses given by participants from both groups?

DESCRIPTION OF PARTICIPANTS

The participants of this study were 23 high school graduates from New York City. They were from two ethnic-national groups: Dominican and Puerto Rican. The Puerto Rican group consisted of 11 students: 6 females and 5 males. The Dominican group consisted of 12 students: 7 females and 5 males. The participants' ages ranged from 18 to 20. The students selected were taking part in an intensive 5-week summer Educational Opportunity Program (EOP) for low socioeconomic status (SES) students. This is a precollege preparation program that stresses study, reading, math, and writing skills. The students were all given the Nelson-Denny standardized reading test as part of the diagnostic procedure to enter the EOP. Both groups had very similar grade-level means in the standardized test. The Puerto Ricans' group mean was 12.6; the Dominicans' group mean was 11.25. This makes the two groups comparable in terms of reading ability. These students were college freshmen at the State University of New York in the fall of 1994. The participants' birthplaces were distributed as shown in Table 3.1.

The participants were given a choice between the English and Spanish languages for interviewing purposes. It must be highlighted that 5 out of 23 participants of the study preferred to be interviewed in Spanish; these 5 students were all Dominicans. Two of these were born in the Dominican Republic, whereas three were born in the United States. Those who preferred to be interviewed in Spanish gave the following

TABLE 3.1

Summary of Participant's Birthplaces

Ethnic/National Group	Number	Birthplace
Puerto Rican	10	United States (New York)
	1	Puerto Rico
Dominican	8	United States (New York)
	4	Dominican Republic

reasons for such preference: "I feel comfortable in both languages," "I like to practice my Spanish whenever I get an opportunity," and "I like to preserve my language."

EDUCATIONAL EXPERIENCES

The educational experiences of the participants from the two groups were somewhat different. Some of the Dominican participants had attended elementary school in the Dominican Republic: two students had studied there 1 year or less, whereas four students had studied 4 to 6 years. All of the Puerto Rican students had studied solely in the United States mainland.

Students' Migration and Travel Experiences

The participants' familial migratory experiences were similar. The majority of the participants were born to parents who had immigrated to the United States. The parents of all the Dominican participants were born in the Dominican Republic. With the exception of two cases, the parents of all the Puerto Rican students were born in Puerto Rico. Of the two parents not born in Puerto Rico, one was born in Spanish Harlem and the other in Guatemala.

All of the participants of the study informed us that they had traveled (Table 3.2). The majority of participants of both groups continued to have contact with their countries of origin. Eight Puerto Ricans reported that they had traveled to Puerto Rico, whereas 11 Dominicans said they had traveled to the Dominican Republic.

Students' Self-Classification. In order to give us an idea of how the students viewed themselves ethnically (personal description), they were asked to classify themselves (see Question 8 in the questionnaire). Of the group, 5 Dominican participants classified themselves as Dominicans, 6 as Dominican Americans, and 1 as an American; whereas 2 Puerto Rican participants classified themselves as Puerto Ricans, 4 as Puerto Rican/Americans, 2 as "Newyorican," 1 as American, and 2 as "other." (These last two classified themselves as Puerto Rican/American plus some other qualification.) As these findings indicate, with the exception of one student from each group, most participants of both groups described themselves as

TABLE 3.2

Travel Experiences of Respondents

Places Traveled	Dominicans	Puerto Ricans
United States only	1	2
United States and Puerto Rico		4
United States and Dominican Republic	7	
United States, Dominican Republic, and Puerto Rico	4	2
United States, Puerto Rico, and Canada		2
Other countries		1
Total	12	11

either a composite of their ethnic background and some other category, or strictly from their ethnic background. This multiplicity of cultural identifications (usually even within an individual) is a direct result of a lived experience as heterogeneous and varied as the cultural identifiers themselves. Note that the Dominican group tended to cluster in two categories—Dominican and Dominican American—whereas the Puerto Rican group showed a wider variability of self-description. This coincides with the Dominican tendency for strong associations between culture and nationality. (See responses to questions later in this chapter.)

The participants were asked to express what it meant for them to be a member of the specific category they chose to describe themselves (see questionnaire). Many of the answers of the Dominican students to this question portrayed a defined sense of belonging—of having rich ethnic and cultural experiences within their communities. Some responses given by these students were:

"I feel proud of my *patria* [fatherland] . . . it is to carry my culture, my language and never forgetting my roots."
"I was born there [the Dominican Republic], my blood is Dominican, my spirit, . . . everything [in me] is Dominican . . . my way of talking . . . of walking. . . .'"
". . . speaking the language, going through the culture, eating the foods, talking with my Dominican friends. . . ."
"Even though I didn't grow up there, I am really like my mom who is a true Dominican. I eat the food, act like them. . . ." (Note here that although this student implies herself to be a true Dominican, she refers to the Dominicans as *them*, therefore excluding herself.)
"I feel that I've been raised as a Dominican. I have adjusted to the American ways because I live here, but my values and everything else comes from the Dominican Republic."

Compared to those of the Dominicans, the answers of some Puerto Rican participants to this question were more brief, less descriptive, and less colorful, with a tendency to view the chosen self-description as a nominal category—that is, a label:

"[Newyorican] is what my mother calls me. It means I have a Puerto Rican background."
"I was born in America and my parents were born in Puerto Rico." [This answer was common among the Puerto Rican participants.]
"It doesn't have a lot of meaning for me, but I do have some pride especially when I am with my family."
"I know a little bit about my culture."

Other Puerto Ricans' responses communicated more tangibly a sense of cultural identity and experience:

"I am 100% Puerto Rican. . . . I think it's to me the best thing, I am proud of who I am. I hope that one day I can live with my people on the Island."
"I have a Puerto Rican background but also a New York attitude incorporated into it."

Notions of Culture and Its Role in the Literary Experience. The participants were asked to define the term *culture.* To evaluate and classify the participants' definitions of culture, we used Williams' (1961) general categories of culture—ideal, documental, and social—but added the category "experiential" for those answers that alluded to the dimension of culture as lived experience.

All participants were able to articulate a description of their notion of culture. Seventeen of them defined the concept by combining more than one category. For example, those who appeared dominated by the ideal category also contained elements of values, religious principles and practices, traditions, social customs, language, clothing, foods; and those who appeared to favor the experiential touched on history, ways of living, and feeling. Such definitions were classified as elaborated. All 17 participants stated directly or implicitly the idea of culture as a way of life. The remaining 6 participants defined the concept of culture as only one of the following aspects: foods, values, clothing, or customs. These definitions were classified as restricted by the researchers. None of the participants made use of the documentary view of culture in answering this question. The participants' responses are summarized in Table 3.3, by ethnic group.

TABLE 3.3

Summary of Students' Concept of Culture

Code	Elaborated	Restricted
Puerto Ricans	9	2
Dominicans	8	4
Total	17	6

Students' Idea of the Culture in the Text. The students were then asked to express their understanding of texts from different cultures. In their answers, the participants demonstrated awareness that there is an implicit culture within the text. That is, the text is a document that records human cultural experience (Williams, 1961). Some of the responses given by the Dominican participants relate the culture in the text with nationality, such as:

"Stories from different peoples, different nationalities with different culture and customs."
"Different authors from different places in the world."
"Texts that talk about people from different countries and their cultures. . . ."

Other responses given by some Dominican participants identify the culture in the text with a way of life, such as:

"Every person where they come from have their own way of life . . . they write about their culture."
"Stories . . . about how other people live."

Finally, some Dominican participants used the notions of perspective and point of view in characterizing the cultural elements in the text. Some examples are:

"Works from different perspectives."
"The themes and points of view of other cultures."

These responses contrast with the answers given by the Puerto Rican participants, which consistently show a tendency to recognize the authorial perspective. Some examples include:

"Different books written from different authors' perspectives."
"Authors that have different ways of living."
"Different stories written by authors from different backgrounds."

These responses, like the responses given by the Dominican participants, made reference to perspectives, ways of life, and backgrounds as descriptors of the culture in the text. However, the concept of nationality did not come about in the responses of the Puerto Rican participants.

Students' Experience With Texts From Other Cultures. When asked if they read text by authors from diverse cultures, 17 participants—10 Dominicans and 7 Puerto Ricans—answered in the affirmative. However, when asked if they understood the texts, only 6 subjects answered in the affirmative: 2 Dominicans and 4 Puerto Ricans. Seven subjects answered in the negative: 4 Dominicans and 3 Puerto Ricans. The remaining 10 subjects answered that they understood them sometimes: 6 Dominicans and 4 Puerto Ricans.

The reasons that the Dominican participants gave for not understanding the texts were as follows:

"The vocabulary is different . . . the way of expression is different."
"Because they have a way of writing that I cannot understand."
"They write about things that I cannot understand."
"There are things they say that I don't understand."

These responses given by Dominican participants indicate that cultural traits such as ways of life, language (vocabulary), and experiences become elements in the text that influence the apprehension of the work of art. The Puerto Rican participants did not specify any particular reasons for not understanding the texts.

The Culture of the Author. Information pertaining to the culture of the author was discerned when students were asked for information that would make a text more comprehensible. The majority of answers given by the participants of both groups indicate that students deem it necessary to know at least some of the author's background, experiences, and motives to understand the literary work. Some of the responses given by participants from both groups were:

"Authors['] background and why they wrote the book."
"Background of the author. I know where he is coming from and the point of view that he's trying to put through."
"To know the author and his or her life . . . where he or she came from and what took him to write the story, his childhood . . . an introduction."
"Knowing about the author, the time period . . . the situation under which the book is being written."
"Why authors are writing a book, what point of view they are trying to get across. . . ."

Analysis of Students' Responses to the Literary Texts. We analyzed the re-sponses given by the participants to the literary texts to ascertain:

1. The influence and/or presence of the students' notions and understanding of culture (restricted vs. elaborated) in the responses to the literary texts.
2. The influence and/or presence of the students' culture (self-categorizations) in the responses to the literary texts.
3. The influence and/or presence of the culture of the text in the participants' responses.

As was mentioned earlier, we asked the students to define the concept of *culture*. We then classified these as elaborated or restricted according to the number of components present in the definitions. We next analyzed the participants' literary responses in order to see if and how their notions of culture—restricted versus elaborated—were reflected in the responses to the texts that they gave.

The analysis indicates that the notion of culture (restricted vs. elaborated) was reflected in two thirds of the responses given by the Dominicans (24 out of 36). Of these, 14 were elaborated and 10 were restricted. In 29 out of 33 responses given by the Puerto Ricans, the notion of culture was also present. Following are some examples to illustrate the students' notion of culture as we found them in the responses given.

A participant of Puerto Rican descent who had described himself as Newyorican and who was classified as to having an elaborated notion of culture responded to the story "Grandmother Spider" by saying, "It was humorous . . . want me to tell you why? (Laughter) It talks about how the culture just sends the biggest and tallest guy to get the fire light and he didn't accomplish it. And so then this little fellow lady called Spider went to get it and she got the fire light or whatever it was."

There are various aspects of this student's cultural sensitivity displayed in his response. For one, he sees the fact of the strong guy being given the task to get the fire as culturally driven: "The culture just sends the biggest and tallest guy to get the fire." Also, in his perception of Grandmother Spider's accomplishment as humorous, this student grasps an element of irony in the event vis-à-vis this culture's presuppositions.

A participant who described herself as Dominican, preferred the Spanish language for interviewing purposes, and whose notion of culture was classified as elaborated, responded to the folktale "People Could Fly": "The story had many different aspects that could be seen. I think that when it spoke about people flying it meant they flew spiritually. When they did witchcraft or something they closed their eyes and they flew. Their spirits flew because from what I know, there is no way that a person can fly."

This participant speaks about "different aspects that could be seen" in the story, although she concentrates on only one. Although this is not explicitly stated in the story, this participant speaks about witchcraft and the meaning it had in the piece. She is unwilling or unable to accept fantasy as a form of literary genre, and resorts to the supernatural to produce her interpretation: "Their spirits flew because, from what I know, there is no way that a human being can fly." Regardless of whether she believed in it or not, she made use of her notions of spiritualism to build her interpretation. The idea of spiritual disembodiment through trance is a common topic in Dominican, Haitian, Puerto Rican, and Cuban spiritualist beliefs.

A participant who classified himself as Dominican American, and who expressed a restricted notion of culture, responded to the poem "T-Bone Steak": "It seems interesting. The comparison of how to make food and how the meat is seasoned." This response is curt and focused on one single aspect—food. The interpretation is strictly literal. In the poem, food can also be interpreted as a symbol standing for many aspects of cultural identity. However, even in this response, we can also see an awareness of the cultural dimension of the text.

A participant who classified herself as Puerto Rican and expressed an elaborated notion of culture described her reaction to the poem "Once to Run" by saying, "I thought this one was deeper. It was harder to understand but I thought it was good. I think it dealt with how people Americanize themselves like, being here they lose their culture. If I had been born in Puerto Rico and grew up there and then brought here it would make me understand more what the person was going through."

In this response we see the student's familiarity with the phenomenon of acculturation—"how people Americanize themselves." This is a result of a personal and collective experience with this phenomenon and the tensions that accompany it. In the last part of her statement she also indicated an awareness of how shared cultural experience facilitates an understanding of the text as a work of art: "If I had been born in Puerto Rico and then brought here it would make me understand more what the person was going through."

The Students' Culture and Response.   The participants were asked to classify themselves and describe what it meant for them to belong to the category chosen. Ten Puerto Rican participants used the category of Puerto Rican in full or in part; 11 Dominican participants used the category of Dominican in full or in part. It was seen, however, that even students who considered themselves purely Puerto Rican or Dominican demonstrated in their responses an awareness of American popular culture.

Let us examine the responses given by some participants. A Puerto Rican participant who described himself as "100% Puerto Rican" described the character of Juan Bobo this way: "He is just clumsy, he is not stupid, he is not dumb, just clumsy." This participant speaks of Juan Bobo as a character of slapstick comedy, a particular North American form of humor. He continued, "They try to make a punch line." This is also an expression used in North American comedy for the understanding of specific forms of humor.

A similar tendency can be seen in the response that a self-classified Dominican gave to the poem "Alone": "I didn't like it. It had a lot of double meaning." This response shows an outward dislike for ambivalence, which may be attributable to a high valuation of directness ("matter-of-factness"), a trait not uncommon to urban life in the United States.

On the other hand, one participant who classified herself as American showed in her response to "The Devil Woman" traits, attitudes, and values commonly associated with a traditional outlook on life: "I liked it because there are some things in life that happen like that . . . and it happened for not listening to what others he cared about told him."

The participant demonstrated a heeding to the elders and acknowledgment of the wisdom of the experienced, because in the story the "others" belong to an older generation. This traditional outlook is influenced by a respect for the "elders" of her own community or a result of a literature curriculum that places too much emphasis on the moral of the story. A combination of both factors is also possible, because they are not mutually exclusive but would tend to reinforce each other.

In the following responses we can see reflected the students' cultures as described by themselves.

A Dominican participant who classified himself as Dominican/American responded to "The Rat In The Wall" with the comment, "I liked it. It shows how superstition can be kind of true." This participant was influenced by a belief in the supernatural. At the same time his choice of words—"kind of true"— shows a noncommittal attitude attributable to the modern urban experience.

Another student was able to capture what Richards (1929) defined as the feeling implicit in the poem in her response to "Alone": "I had to read it a couple of times and I still think I didn't understand it fully. . . . I would like to have known what specifically was he talking about . . . because I saw two perspectives in it: that of a person who's locked up and that of a person in another country."

Because she couldn't immediately perceive the literal meaning of the words, she concluded that her understanding is deficient. In demanding a straightforward understanding she might be demonstrating a discomfort with ambivalence characteristic of "urban pragmatism." But she apprehended and responded to the feeling of isolation in the poem. Her depiction of this feeling was expressed as "a person in another country." Here she was encountering echoes of her community's experience with migration.

Another participant who had described himself as Puerto Rican/American responded as follows to the folktale "Juan Bobo": "I saw at the end of the story . . . my parents told me something like that, they told me a story of Juan Bobo and they would always call me lazy . . . she used to call me Juan Bobo."

One element of his cultural experience reflected in the response is the fact that he was told the story when he was a child, and was even called Juan Bobo. It's common in Puerto Rico to use this epithet jokingly with young people.

Culture as Lived Experience.   The qualities of vividness, intensity, and engagement manifested by some students in their answers were treated as an index of the sense they have of their own culture as lived experience (enthusiasm, specific wording, and reference to personal experience were used as indicators). Although we cannot conclude that this sense does not exist just because a person is not able to articulate it, we examined the literary responses of those students that had previously manifested a clear sense of culture as lived experience to see if it was also reflected in their responses. Following are some examples in which students were responding to the poem, "Napa, California."

"It explains how they were working . . . in little plantations . . . they were working in the hot sun; it seemed like if they were in slavery . . . it explains what they were doing but at the same time allowing me to enter their minds . . . like Oh God what should we do . . . no matter how hard the job is, they keep going because they know there is a better life." This response demonstrates the hope for a better way of living which resembles her community's lived experience.

A student responded to "The Devil Woman" like this: "That one is really true . . . there are some things in the world that people cannot explain . . . this one is true. I can relate to this kind [of story] because everybody has their own personal devils . . . I have seen the devil in dreams . . . and I can relate to that. . . ." The archetypal figure of the devil is a very relevant icon of Puerto Rican and Dominican Catholicism. The participant can relate to the character of the devil in this Mexican folktale.

A student responds to the poem "Theme for English B": "That one I liked a lot because it brings you home right to New York . . . Langston Hughes lived in Harlem in 1920, 1930 and I wish I could be back there . . . even though it was hard and all . . . as I read the poem I could see myself right in the window at night, and I could see the lights, it reminds me of home." This response coincides with the students self-categorization as Puerto Rican/American. It shows that he is very much in contact with his lived urban experience and can use it to create a meaningful and vivid reading experience.

The Culture of the Text and Response.   As we discussed earlier, many students from both groups demonstrated an awareness of the fact that the text portrayed a specific culture that was not necessarily their own. The responses of the Dominican students reflected the culture of the texts in 13 cases. That is, they saw the text as portraying specific beliefs, values, and experiences of human groups. Some also see their own cultural experiences echoing in the text. In 26 cases, the Dominican responses did not reflect the culture of the text. On the other hand, the Puerto Rican responses reflected the culture of the text in 21 cases and was absent in 12 cases.

Following are some examples as students respond to "Juan Bobo":

"It is a typical story because it was like a story that is told to all children when they are little about mischievous kids that do bad things for not listening to their parents." This was a Dominican student's response indicates a view of text as cultural artifact, or documentary.

"It brought back memories. . . . The way they told it [in my hometown]." This Puerto Rican subject had heard the story in Spanish; he spoke about the purpose of folktales. He responded with categories of lived experience, documentary, and cultural artifact.

"Very interesting; very educational and funny . . . from all the stories I read the one I best understood was the story of Juan Bobo because it explains, it talks about 'Batey.' I know what it is and it makes it easier for me to understand" (text as lived experience and documentary).

A student responded to "Napa California": "It explains how they were working . . . in little plantations . . . they were working in the hot sun; it seemed like if they were in slavery" (text as documentary).

DISCUSSION AND IMPLICATIONS

As can be seen, not only do the participants demonstrate an awareness/knowledge of the concept of culture (even if restricted in some instances), but in many cases, when speaking about their own cultures, this awareness (or "metacognition of culture") comes through as a very concrete experiential reality in the lives of these students. Upon examining the students' responses to the literary texts it was evident that in many of them this knowledge, awareness, and vividness carried over to the response. Two texts were very salient: the urban experience ("Alone," "Theme for English B"), and the multiculturalism and acculturation experiences ("T-Bone Steak," "Once to Run," "Yellow Woman").

At the same time, in their reactions to the folk tales, especially "Juan Bobo," the students showed to be very much in touch with cultural elements of Puerto Rico and Santo Domingo. Of particular interest are those elements that can be catalogued as cross-cultural universals: respect for the elders, the dignity of work and effort even under exploitation, the spiritual and supernatural, and the value of justice. Most participants demonstrated an awareness of the text as a cultural manifestation. This was verified in many of the responses. Again, this was most evident in poems that expounded the multicultural experience.

We acknowledge, after conducting this study, the complexity of the concept of culture and the difficulty of extracting it from literary response. In observing cultural groups it is important to look not only at institutions, behaviors, interactions, values, and ideas, but also at what these mean in terms of lived experiences, or how these shape people's quality of life. In the specific case of members of groups that have been "transplanted" to the United States mainland, it is worthwhile to examine their years of residence in this country. If the subject is a student, years of schooling in the United States mainland will most likely influence many aspects of that person's cultural makeup. It may also be noteworthy to keep in mind that what we call *culture* could in fact be a plurality of backgrounds within a single individual. As one student put it when responding to the poem "T-Bone Steak," "People make distinctions on physical differences, they don't really look at the cultural differences or what's underlying."

The factors mentioned previously are key for understanding readers' responses as was observed all throughout this study. This and the coincidence of aims between the study of literature and multiculturalism argue very strongly in favor of the development of curricula that incorporate both fields. Finally, of utmost importance is the fact that students should not all be lumped into general rubrics such as "Hispanic" because basic differences underlie the groups.

The nature and purpose of this study—to find the best ways to present multicultural texts to students—prompted us to ask the students for their recommendations. What follows are some of the responses given by participants from both cultural groups in an effort to make literature teaching/learning a more relevant activity.

"First, teachers should do a book survey. Second, a book should be interesting. Teachers should give background information on the writer, the era in which it was written and the people it represents. Third, the teachers should make it fun for the kids to read because if they don't find it fun they're not going to read it."

"Before a story is presented to me I would like to know about the author. And if the story is presented to me, it should not only be that poem or story. It should also be other selections because what about if like in high school teachers give you just one poem from that author and they expect you to interpret it and there are other views that the author has . . . by reading selections, maybe an autobiography one can interpret the stories."

"In a simple way, I think it should be simple and straight to the point so a reader can understand no matter where they come from."

". . . that deal with real life experiences."

"For some texts the writers' information and comments on the texts can help me understand it better."

It is important to note that these comments were from high school graduates. Many of these students from both groups made an emphasis on the need of having some basic information on the authors' backgrounds in order to have a better understanding of the texts. Their suggestions also imply that they like to be involved in the text selection procedure. To see what teachers report about their practices and problems in presenting multicultural literature, we now turn to the second phase of the study, presented in the next chapter.

4

Teaching Multicultural Literature

❧ ◆ ❧

Steven Ostrowski

This chapter focuses on approximately 25 teachers from secondary schools across the United States who regularly use multicultural literature in their classrooms. These teachers were recommended by a variety of supervisors, researchers, and administrators, and in turn the teachers agreed to participate in the study. They teach in schools in New York, New Jersey, Kansas, Montana, California, and Hawaii. All but one teach in public schools.

The information we generated came from periodic long-answer survey questions, extensive annual end-of-year reports, telephone and e-mail exchanges, and interviews. Seven of the teachers in the project presented papers and engaged in round-table discussions of their work at the annual NCTE convention in San Diego in November 1995. Although the participation of a few of the teachers in the project was spotty and inconsistent, most participants regularly answered our questions and wrote detailed and conscientious summer reports. Some teachers went beyond our expectations, keeping us up to date with new materials and texts they had discovered, as well as by sending us lesson plans, examples of essay questions and students' written responses to them, students' reports, and less formal but often highly relevant anecdotes from day-to-day happenings in their classrooms. As Alan Purves noted in his introductory letter to participating teachers, and as will become clear as you read this chapter, the real authors of this portion of the study are the teachers themselves.

Although some of the information we provide may not be new to those familiar with issues surrounding the teaching of multicultural literature, some of it will be. This is because most of what is presented here describes the actual experiences of practitioners, and is not overly concerned with theories and musings of academics who are sometimes far removed from the classroom, especially the secondary classroom. In this report, we are only concerned with theory insofar as the teachers themselves are or are not concerned with it. Thus, from the start, the long-answer survey questions we sent to participating teachers were quite broad in scope. The questions made few assumptions. Following are some examples of the types of questions with which we began our study:

Why do you teach multicultural literature?
How are you going about teaching multicultural texts?
How do you choose the texts you use?
How do you feel your students are responding to them?
What difficulties are you encountering and from what quarters do these difficulties come?
What successes are you enjoying?
What personal insights are you gaining?

As our research team read and discussed the initial responses to these and similar questions, we saw trends emerge, but were also at times surprised by unanticipated responses. We discovered that teachers had very different approaches to teaching multicultural literature, different philosophies about it, and different overall styles of teaching as well as reporting to us about it.

In an attempt to maintain a dialogue with the teachers, our further questions and occasional comments became at times more specific and pointed than the initial ones, and at other times more general, more philosophically oriented, or more practical. Sometimes the same question was asked several times over the course of the years. Although we weren't able to offer as much individual follow-up to teachers as we (and they) would have liked, when we did personalize correspondence, the exchanges usually proved mutually beneficial. I should admit here, however, that a few teachers occasionally found some of our questions redundant, ill-informed, or even naive. We learned as much from those critiques as from other kinds of responses.

In all, we accumulated hundreds of pages of documents that reflect the thoughts and describe the actions of a group of highly dedicated educators involved in a wide range of pedagogical issues around the teaching of multicultural literature. The documents testify to the fact that, for teachers who do teach multicultural literature (and, as Applebee, 1990, showed, the majority of English and language arts teachers don't), it is a vibrant, frustrating, eye-opening, sometimes volatile, and, at the dawn of the twenty-first century, increasingly necessary endeavor.

LITERATURE INSTRUCTION IN THE UNITED STATES: A BRIEF OVERVIEW

In the United States, English emerged as a major school subject at the end of the nineteenth century. It pulled together the studies of, among other things, reading, literary history, composition, grammar, spelling, and oratory. From the very beginning, however, literature was the primary focus of the English program, in particular the literature of Great Britain and the United States. Through the years, because of various new demands put on the English program, redefinitions have come about as to what students should learn from the literature they study, but rarely has literature's essential place in the program been challenged (Applebee, 1990, 1994). Furthermore, literature from the United States (rightly so) and Great Britain continue to be the primary focus in most classrooms.

In a wide-ranging study entitled "Literature Instruction in American Schools," Applebee (1990) found that the largest percentage of time in the typical English or language arts classroom continues to be dedicated to the study of literature. This is true of all three of the high school populations (public, private, and Catholic) he studied. But what, or should we say, whose, literature is being taught and studied? How are literary texts being chosen? What, if any, literary theories are teachers using to help inform them in their choices of texts?

It may please some and dismay others to know that Applebee found that traditional texts are still very much alive in most of America's high school English classrooms. In fact, Applebee's study showed that "The overall emphasis in the curriculum remains on selections by White, male authors from an Anglo-Saxon tradition" (1990, p. 58). Importantly, in most cases decisions to teach these texts are being made by teachers themselves. Only 5% of teachers responding reported being given little or no leeway in the selections they taught, whereas 30% claimed to have complete freedom of choice. Most teachers faced some constraints, such as recommended departmental reading lists and limited budgets, but generally they reported being not unhappy with the selection of texts available to them, even though the selection lists tended to favor traditional, "canonical" texts.

Clearly, factors beyond the limitations imposed by departmental policies and budgets are needed to explain why so many English teachers continue to teach primarily traditional texts. An overwhelming majority of Applebee's teachers (92% of public school teachers) rated literary merit as the most important criterion for text selection. (The teachers of multicultural literature whom we studied concurred with this.) Because most teachers also reported unfamiliarity with many multicultural texts, it stands to reason that those texts they found to possess the greatest literary merit derived from the traditions with which they were most familiar.

Teachers, particularly public school teachers, also reported that they worried about community reaction to nontraditional texts. This is somewhat surprising, because public schools are more likely than private and Catholic schools to have diverse student populations. Thus,

> [Teachers'] reports suggest that when it comes to broadening the canon to include more works by women and minorities, teachers may be unsure of the literary merit of new selections, personally unfamiliar with them (thus making them initially less teachable), and worried about community reaction—and as a result the curriculum changes with glacial slowness. (Applebee, 1990, p. 67)

Although Applebee's study did not deal directly with the question of the influence of literary theory on teachers' choices of texts, it did deal with theory's influence on teacher goals. Although some constructivist thought, for example, can be detected in some of these goals, particularly in the form of a reader-response approach to literature, the majority of English teachers continue to operate primarily from what might be called a reading comprehension-type approach, as the results described in the previous two chapters attest. Additionally, although many teachers profess to lead "student-centered" classrooms and rate that concept highly, in practice their classrooms tend to be organized around a more or less traditional, text-centered paradigm.

Another, and perhaps more penetrating, set of explanations for the continued teaching of traditional texts is to be found in the various essays in Miller and

McCaskill (1993). They included such facts and attributions as access to inexpensive material, allegiance to the pieces of literature taught to them in college, a general resistance to change from effective practices and works that have been "teachable," confusion about where to go and what to add, and pressure from the community.

Thus, the typical high school English classroom looks something like this: It is comprised of culturally diverse students and a White teacher. The teacher, under certain departmental constraints as well as for personal, social, and perhaps philosophical and psychological reasons, uses mostly traditional texts, such as the works of Shakespeare and Hemingway, in teaching literature. The teacher employs to some extent reader-response techniques with his or her students, and believes in the concept of the student-centered classroom, but essentially his or her teaching of literature (and, by extrapolation, his or her choices of literary texts) is organized around a traditional reading comprehension-type model. All in all, in the past 50 years relatively little has changed in the way literature instruction in America's secondary schools has been carried out.

But what about those teachers who do, or at least attempt to, challenge the "silences" and change the curriculum by emphasizing multicultural literature in their classrooms? It is to those individuals and to an examination of their goals, methods, strategies, philosophies, failures, and successes that we now turn.

TEACHERS TEACHING MULTICULTURAL LITERATURE

What is culture? What is the difference between ethnicity and culture? Between nationality and culture? Between culture and counterculture? What is a subculture? Are we all influenced, and hence members of or participants in, only one primary culture, or are we a part of many cultures at the same time? If the latter, is the word *multicultural* redundant? In an early meeting of our research team, Alan Purves asked if we weren't all multicultural beings. We agreed that we were. Subsequently, we have heard from many teachers who have asked similar questions and come up with similar answers. Nevertheless, they continue to teach courses in "multicultural" literature, which are seen as quite distinct from, say, courses called "American Literature" or "British Literature" or even "World Literature."

Under dissimilar circumstances, in different settings, several of the teachers in our study independently reported coming to moments of sincere "confusion" and "difficulty" in the past few years when confronting the concepts of culture and multiculturalism. These "confrontations" seem to have been precipitated by the growing use, particularly the pedagogical use, of the more recent (and more recently popular) of these terms. The frequency of the use of the term *multiculturalism* has caused many teachers (and perhaps many people in general) to reexamine the nature of culture itself. After all, the teachers' reasoning seems to go, if you are professing to teach students multicultural literature, you ought to be able to be clear about just what culture itself is. For English teacher Judy Maltz, the "crisis" came in a course she herself was taking, when the instructor asked each of the students to describe his or her own culture. Judy was struck by how difficult this question was to answer, and it became more difficult when the instructor further asked that the students describe how they think others perceive their culture, whatever their "culture" might be. Our group of teachers from Kansas, in collectively answering a question we'd asked about what cultural groups they were discussing in their classes, replied, "What is culture? The nature of culture is not easy for the kids or us. . . . Teachers lack clarity about what culture is. There is also a lot of cultural misunderstanding and misinformation, e.g., kids don't recognize that Egyptians are also Africans."

Another teacher, Joyce Greenberg Lott, related how a search through some recent and supposedly high-quality educational software for the term *multiculturalism* proved fruitless. When she then looked up the word *culture*, she discovered the following "categories": gentility, customs, education, experience, and society—broad, to say the least. Pursuing a mini-research project of her own in which she followed some of the trails of the various categories of "culture," and also looking into other sources including journal reports and newspaper articles for information about multiculturalism, Joyce concluded that both terms, although used rather pointedly in political arguments by people of all persuasions, are otherwise woefully imprecise.

A final example illustrates with some local specificity the problems teachers can have with these imprecise terms. Our team of teachers from Hawaii wrote to us of their struggle to determine what "the" culture is on those islands, given the diversity of inhabitants, which include Chinese, Filipinos, Native Hawaiians, Samoans, Tongans, and Whites. (Regarding the latter, the teachers took care to note that the cultural distinction had shifted from ethnicity to race—a further complication of the issue.) The Hawaiian teachers also pointed out that their own "culture" differed, for example, from the culture of their parents, as well as from that (or should I say those?) of their students. How, the teachers wanted to know, were they to deal with our questions about multiculturalism and culture under these circumstances? At the very least, we were not to hope for simple, unambiguous answers.

It should be made clear from the start that although I speak throughout this chapter of multicultural literature and of culture, I, as researcher, never do define these terms here, because to do so would be to impose assumptions that the teachers whom I am studying may not have made. Instead, by tolerating the ambiguity of the terms, I hope to learn something about them and about the people who use them.

Multicultural Literature and Teachers' Goals

It is hard to imagine any teacher being effective in the classroom without having clear goals for him- or herself as a teacher and for his or her students as learners. There are many levels of goals, however. Most teachers share certain general goals, for example the goal of having the majority of one's students not only "pass" a class but learn to think and reason well, and perhaps truly to come to understand and enjoy a given subject. There are also more specific teacher goals, such having each student in a class compose an original haiku and submit it to a schoolwide literary journal. Goals are obviously important; they can reveal much about the philosophy and priorities of a teacher.

We asked our teachers about their goals with respect to teaching multicultural literature. Why did they teach it? What was their vision for their students?

Teachers' responses tended to fall broadly into three categories, although other significant but less general goals were also mentioned. The first broad category contained goals that had to do with what might be called "difference" issues. That is, most of the teachers in the study said that through the teaching of multicultural literature they hoped to have their students come to understand, appreciate, and respect people of other cultures. Here are some examples of this type of response:

"Strengthening their ability to truly respect the other as fellow homo sapiens."
"I feel that schools must teach some values and one of the most important is respecting others."
"These students will live and work in a 'multi' society—I want them to be able to act and interact in diverse groups—without offending."
"I wanted to help all my students to know that all cultures and ethnic groups have riches to contribute to our classroom and to society."

A significant majority of the respondents mentioned some form of "difference" issues as a major goal for their classes.

The second goal comprised responses that emphasized "similarity" issues. That is, teachers hoped through the teaching of multicultural literature to have students come to recognize the universality of all people, to see all people as comprising one "human family," and to find and emphasize fundamental aspects of being that all humans share. Roughly half of the respondents included this as an important goal. Here are some representative quotes:

"I [try] to make the novel universal by relating the main character's growth to students' own growth and search for self-identity."
"Through reading, I hope that [my students] will understand that different people are not threatening. They may be just like themselves in many ways."
"I teach literature from other cultures because I believe in the premise that we are all alike despite our differences. I want my students to learn this also."

Goals emphasizing cultural differences and goals emphasizing cultural similarities are not mutually exclusive, of course, and many teachers wrote of wanting their students to see both the fundamental needs and tendencies that all human beings share, that is, the need for love and companionship, the need for rituals and myths, the need to form social units, and so on, as well as the different cultural forms that these fundamental needs and tendencies take.

Not all teachers, or groups of teachers, saw both these goals as equally important, however. For example, Bryant Fillion, the site coordinator for the Kansas teachers, summarized a major issue discussed at a meeting of the group: "There was general agreement that teachers need to stress similarities of people and events depicted in literature to students' own experiences, because students themselves concentrate, sometimes exclusively, on differences and negatives. Kids [already] tend to be critical and judgmental and often hostile to differences."

A third, related goal, mentioned less often than the first two but nevertheless with some regularity, was that of using literary works from the students' own cultures with the hope of building students' self-esteem and developing pride in their ethnic cultures. In certain schools in Montana, for example, where significant numbers of the students are Native Americans, goals related to building self-esteem were rated quite highly.

Another goal expressed by several teachers, and that was of particular concern to Dorothea Susag who teaches just outside an Indian reservation in Montana, was "the desire to erase stereotyping through education and understanding." Dorothea and other teachers recognized a tendency in their students, in other teachers, and often in authors, to resort quickly and unthinkingly to stereotyping. They hoped to eradicate this kind of automatic thinking through literature. "Eradication" often meant reading both works that did not portray minorities in stereotypical ways as well as works that did. In literature that perpetuated stereotypes, the goal was to teach students to identify and discuss the stereotyping: Why was a certain character portrayal a stereotype? How do stereotypes come about? Is there any truth in the stereotype? What is the danger of stereotyping? Dorothea, whose classes consist of both Native and non-Native Americans and who teaches a great deal of Native American literature, commented, "We look for values, belief systems, and human behaviors which the literature reveals. Then students look for consistencies and disparities with their previous knowledge about Indian peoples and their experiences."

Finally, the "main objective" of Marge Abbott, who also teaches many Native American students, was to encourage lifelong reading habits and to "widen the horizons of students who may not venture out of the reservation very often."

Teaching Strategies (or, How to Achieve Teaching Goals)

Goals imply strategies. As we have seen, multicultural literature and language arts teachers wish to promote a healthy respect for cultural differences as well as an appreciation for the similarities underlying all cultures. At the same time, they try to raise the self-esteem of minority students without alienating "majority" students. How do they do it?

Choosing Multicultural Texts.   I deliberately include here, at the beginning of the Teaching Strategies section, the issue of how and why teachers choose the texts they choose, because choice of text cannot legitimately be separated from either teaching goals or teaching strategies, even when, as is sometimes the case, texts are mandated by departments or districts. Choice of text is particularly important in multicultural literature classes where, fairly or unfairly, individual texts are often weighted with the responsibility of "representing" the cultures from which their authors come. (I discuss this problem in more detail later.)

How, then, do multicultural literature teachers choose texts? What constraints do they face regarding text selection? The most commonly cited sources in our study were anthologies, which have the advantage of giving teachers a fairly wide range of choice in a single volume. (On the down side, some teachers and students complained that anthologies' sizes could be real physical burdens.) Some of the specific anthologies teachers mentioned as good ones are *Braided Lives*, *Literature and Language*, *Growing Up Chicano*, *World Literature* (Prentice-Hall), *Multicultural Perspectives*, and *World Masterpieces*. Of these, *Braided Lives* was both the most commonly cited as well as the most highly praised, for its variety and quality of selections. The full-length works the teachers cite as being "successes" in their classrooms include such diverse titles as: *The Joy Luck Club, Things Fall Apart, Siddhartha, Sound of Waves, Bless Me Ultima, The Bluest Eye, Their Eyes Were Watching God, Invisible Man, I Know Why the Caged Bird Sings, El Norte, Kafir Boy, Black Boy, The Light in the Forest, Inherit the Wind,* and *Hunger of Memory.*

For some teachers, text choices were mandated by their departments. Choices were also limited in some cases by department bookroom inventories, particularly regarding longer works. Some teachers who were restricted by inventories were allowed to choose shorter works such as poems, short stories, and essays from wherever they might find them, and use department photocopying equipment to make multiple copies.

When budgets allowed, teachers sought out new works. As sources for titles they mentioned word of mouth, conferences such as those conducted by NCTE, in-service meetings, magazines such as *The English Journal,* and book reviews. In the Appendix to this volume is a partial list of some of the full-length works teachers in our study have chosen for use in their classes. Some of these are mentioned later in this section, when we detail a few of the specific teaching strategies that teachers employ.

Literary Quality as a Factor in Choosing Multicultural Texts

Some critics have charged that in the interest of "inclusion," literary quality is being sacrificed in those classrooms that emphasize a multicultural approach to the teaching of literature. According to these critics, teachers feel that as long as they have on their teaching "menus" a smattering of Eastern literature, a touch of Latin American, a taste of African, and so on, then they're doing what they're supposed to do. Furthermore, an examination of the teacher goals described previously might suggest that most teachers perceive their mission, if you will, in teaching multicultural literature as one of having students come to acknowledge, understand, and even celebrate the diversity of peoples and cultures that comprise our world and our school populations. This approach appears to use literature as a tool for shaping or changing society rather than as a primarily aesthetic object that, if it shapes or changes society, does so with some degree of subtlety.

Our study, however, reveals that teachers care very deeply that the works they choose possess literary merit, or "quality" as they themselves are wont to say, that they are indeed aesthetic objects, and that not any work, merely because it derives from the culture currently being studied, will suffice. As English teacher Myrna Steele said, "I attempt to select quality pieces of literature that contain elements with which students can personally identify, and hopefully, that give them a new insight into themselves and/or their environment." Mary Carter wrote, "A good story is a good story. But the fact that the story comes from a culture different from my own does color and deepen the enjoyment." Gloria Lewis stated that she told her AP students that they studied multicultural literature for the same reasons they studied any other literature, except that a little more emphasis was placed on "understanding and appreciation of others' cultures and values." Stacie Valdez succinctly put it this way: "I choose those pieces that are excellent pieces of literature." She went on to express her own growing reservations about the use of the term *multicultural literature,* saying that the term tended to give the literature "token status." Valdez went on, "I teach literature that reflects society. I don't select a piece of literature because the piece was written by an author from a different culture, [but] because it is well written, has a message relevant for the unit, and is written at a level that my students will be able to understand and find meaning in."

Even for those teachers who don't directly mention it in their responses, in many cases it may be that literary quality is simply taken for granted as a criterion for text selection. In fact, one teacher said as much when she wrote in answer to a question regarding literary quality in text selection that she needn't address the issue of aesthetics because "Literature implies aesthetics." Throughout their correspondences with us, teachers spoke passionately of their love of literature and of language. Far from being politically dogmatic, the teachers saw in all kinds of literature a rich source of wisdom, power, and pleasure. Here is teacher Marge Abbott's description of literature and its value:

> [Literature] is a message in a bottle thrown into an ocean of time and space. It widens the reader's horizons. It excites the reader's emotions and imagination. It can be an historical signpost. It is the best tool for teaching understanding and acceptance of people of other faiths, colors, nations. It can be inspirational, motivating the reader to strive for excellence. It is a temporary mask behind which the reader can experience other lives.

I venture to state that most, if not all, of our teachers were and continue to be unwilling to teach "just any old text" so long as it is somehow "multicultural." To the extent possible (and as I have shown, there were limitations) choices were made with literary quality (as the teachers themselves defined "quality") being a high—and often the highest—priority.

Problems With Choosing Texts. One of the major problems teachers face in choosing multicultural texts is their relative unfamiliarity with literary works of other cultures, particularly works of cultures whose literary presence in the United States to date has been minimal, except perhaps to specialists. Certainly in their own education, most teachers did not have the opportunity, after extensive study of American and British literature, to get too far beyond the traditional classics of world literature.

Given that they will not settle for any work of literature simply because its cultural context fits their needs, teachers are forced in the course of their typically heavy daily schedules to search for, buy (often with their own money), read, and try to determine the appropriateness of various works of literature from different cultures and sometimes different historical periods. (In this respect, teachers for whom multicultural works are mandated might feel a certain relief from an unwanted burden. However, in cases where teachers are not satisfied with mandated works, they may wish they had the burden despite the extra work it entails.)

Teachers also stated discomfort with the idea of a single piece of literature being used to "represent" a culture. They were often unsure if a work they were using or considering would accurately portray life in a given culture. They weren't always certain if the actions of important characters were typical or atypical of persons in a given cultural context. "How do we know," Norma Couchman and Linda Hoobler, team-teachers from Kansas, wrote, "if the particular selections are really 'representative' if we don't know much about the culture? How do we know if the presentations are stereotypes?" Teachers reported sometimes relying on the first-hand knowledge of students of the culture being studied, but again questions arose as to whether an individual student or even a group of students could speak in any objective way for an entire culture.

A few teachers voiced as a problem having to find materials that would not be offensive to one or more students or groups of students. Religious and/or sexually explicit subject matter was mentioned as potentially offensive by one teacher, who concluded "Choices must be made with care and taste and presented as literature only." (The teacher did not elaborate, and we unfortunately missed the opportunity to ask her to do so, on exactly what she meant by "presented as literature only.")

Another problem some of our teachers mentioned was that of providing "equal time" for all cultures and points of view. But what does *equal* mean here? Does it mean literally spending the same amount of time on each work from each culture? Is it determined by how many students from a given culture are in the class for any one semester? Does it necessitate, for example, treating short poems or short stories from one culture with the same depth of analysis as long novels or full-length plays from another, all in the interest of fairness and equality? The Kansas group expressed the problem this way: "It's unclear to what extent we should gear courses to the students who are there. If you have five countries or cultures represented in a class, do you try to include literature from all five countries?"

Although it would seem that there might be some commonsense solutions to some of these issues, they can nevertheless pose real problems for conscientious teachers and culturally sensitive students.

For Linda Hoobler and Norma Couchman, the whole enterprise of teaching multicultural literature was so new and untried that they felt they had to literally "invent the curriculum." Inventing a curriculum is time- and energy-consuming, even for those whose full-time job it is to do so. For teachers whose days include all manner of additional responsibilities and obligations, it can be overwhelming.

Below are some additional—and typical—responses to questions about problems with finding and/or choosing multicultural texts.

> "The biggest problem is finding titles, then finding the time to read them to decide whether they would be of interest to students" (Gloria Lewis).
> "Certain cultures in my class have not had any representative literature read. For example, I don't know any Korean stories, or African other than Achebe" (Mary Carter).
> "I feel it is critical for students to know something about the author. I often have a very difficult time finding even minimal biographical information on many authors from other cultures" (Stacie Valdez).
> "I battle a lack of confidence and true knowledge about the culture" (Kansas group).
> "We have to provide extensive cultural and historical background. It is very difficult to find and very disjointed" (Kansas group).

These comments point to problems of adequate time, resources, and back-ground. They point to opportunities for publishers, librarians, and preservice and in-service instructors. It is noted that some of these concerns mirror those of English and language arts teachers generally, as reported by Applebee (1990) and discussed earlier. Our study, like Applebee's, found that teachers—in our case, teachers already committed to teaching multicultural literature—had significant reservations about their own ability to teach multicultural literature, as well as serious questions about the literary quality of literature with which they were often unfamiliar. However, one concern that Applebee's subjects reported that the majority of our teachers found not to be a problem was that of parental and community reaction to multicultural literature. By and large, our teachers said that they either had no reaction whatsoever from parents or the community regarding their choices of literature (not necessarily a good thing), or else they felt that they had the support of parents and of the larger community (a very good thing). Particularly supportive of multicultural efforts were Native American parents, who—as teachers who taught Native American students told us—were happy to see their traditional literature being read and discussed in the schools.

Although there were few serious negatives raised by teachers regarding parental/community reaction to texts and/or culture, one group of teachers did write that they were concerned that some of the parents of their students were very biased about different cultures (they cited as an example some Asian parents' biases against African Americans). "The kids," they wrote, "may handle it well in the classroom, but homes may be extremely biased racially . . . parents not wanting teachers to teach children not to be racially biased. The kids are OK and excited about cultural studies, opening it up, but the parents may resent this." But as we discuss later, sometimes the kids themselves are not "OK" about cultural studies either.

The most serious problem we heard of regarding parental reaction to a work resulted in the censoring of Montanan and Native American author James Welch's *Winter in the Blood*. The parents of one student objected to the book's "language and promiscuity" and brought their complaint to a district supervisor, who agreed that the book went too far. "The book was not censured for its multicultural quality, thank goodness," the teacher wrote, "but my students did address the issue of White guilt and how this book did have the tendency to blame the dominant culture for [its Native American protagonist's] woes."

STRATEGIES FOR TEACHING MULTICULTURAL TEXTS

In this section we look at some of the ways teachers introduce and then teach multicultural texts to their students. We were interested in knowing whether the teaching of these texts is done in more or less traditional ways, or if the nature of the texts, and their contexts, mean finding new ways of presentation and engagement. We also look at the issue of assessment to see if multicultural literature learning is assessed differently from that of traditional literature learning.

Providing Background Information

We asked teachers what information beyond that given in the text itself they felt it necessary to provide to their students as scaffolding for multicultural texts. Most teachers responded that they sought out whatever background information they could about such things as the author, the author's culture, the culture with which the piece dealt, and the culture from which the piece was derived. In general, teachers felt that background information was essential to a fuller understanding of a work of multicultural literature. For example, Donna Miller wrote, "The challenge is in the history beyond the text. If the text is the only authority, the richness is limited—backgrounds require research."

As has already been discussed and illustrated, some teachers expressed great difficulty in finding relevant cultural background information. This often required extensive searching and expenditure of time. Information about everything from Jim Crow laws and the general historical conditions for African Americans in early- to mid-twentieth-century America to politics in nineteenth-century China to the origins of various Native American creation myths had to be provided in such a way that it made sense to students and aided their comprehension of and appreciation for the work they were about to study.

Teachers did their best to find other resources to enhance the literature they were going to teach. Daniel Smith reported that background information to literary works he's done with his classes has been provided by guest speakers from India and Japan, speakers whom his department helped him to procure. Dorothea Susag had a Blackfeet storyteller and oral historian speak to her classes. In keeping with Native American custom, her students were told not to bring notebooks and pens to class that day, but simply to respectfully listen. Susag wrote, "I had never seen the students so quiet and attentive." In order to provide background information on Hinduism and Buddhism (the class was about to read *Siddhartha*), one teacher invited Hindus from the school to come and speak to her classes. She also had a women come in to lead the students in yoga, and took the students on a trip to a Buddhist Temple. Furthermore, she paraphrased some Confucian sayings and asked students to state whether or not they agreed with premises of the sayings. Before studying the play *Inherit the Wind*, Judith Maltz had her class study and discuss a host of creation stories from various cultures. They also reviewed Darwin's theories, as well as some of the evidence they found to support them.

Other teachers use maps and atlases, computers, films, and recordings to enhance lessons about various cultures. Several of our teachers worked in multidisciplinary teams in conjunction with teachers of subjects such as history, geography, and religion. Most, although not all, of these arrangements proved worthwhile and fruitful.

Overall, in most cases reported to us, students did not begin a literary work until they'd already studied the geography and at least some of the history of a given culture, although in some cases, for various pedagogical reasons, teachers reported deliberately withholding cultural information before a reading in order to get at and then analyze students' raw reactions to a piece. Background information was also provided, in many cases, throughout the study of a work as was deemed appropriate or necessary by the teacher.

WAYS OF LOOKING AT TEXTS

There are many ways that teachers and students of literature look at texts. Following are descriptions of some of the ways teachers reported looking at multicultural texts with their students.

Thematically

When asked how they were looking at multicultural texts, many, indeed most, of the teachers we corresponded with reported that they took (at least some of the time) a thematic approach. This is a quite traditional approach, one that many English and language arts teachers take regardless of the type of literature they are teaching. In the case of our teachers, however, most believed using a thematic approach was the best route to reaching their overall goals for teaching multicultural literature.

Taking a thematic approach allowed teachers to integrate traditional works with newer, or unfamiliar, multicultural ones. Several teachers noted that the thematic approach was conducive to achieving the goals of examining and coming to understand cultural similarities and differences. For example, Barbara King-Shaver connects Western and non-Western works by theme. In one of her units, called "The Hero's Quest," she teaches *Beowulf* side by side with *Gilgamesh*, *The Odyssey* side by side with *The Mahabharata*, *Their Eyes Were Watching God* side by side with *Siddhartha*.

Teachers also felt that "universal themes" found in the literature could be related profitably to the students' own lives. "One reason I always teach thematically," said Stacie Valdez in an interview I conducted with her at the NCTE convention in San Diego, "is, I don't want to emphasize, well, this is a Black kid who's experiencing loneliness, I want [my students] to be able to see, wow, his loneliness is similar to when I've been lonely, even though in some ways he's different." Myrna Steele teaches thematically because it is important that students see how similar we all really are. She believes it is a particularly egregious mistake to teach multicultural literature in blocks—this is African literature, this is American literature, this is Asian literature—for the very reason that it tends to point to differences as opposed to the commonalities that she finds most important to emphasize. Mark Zaminski, in explaining why he chose to take a thematic approach, said he felt it was "good for analysis." He added that it also helped foster "high [student] interest."

Some of the specific themes that teachers mentioned using in teaching literary units were "Heros and Heroism," "Coming of Age/Rites of Passage," "Stereotype and Bias," "Maturity," "Inclusion/Exclusion," "Perspectives," "Cultural Identity," "Racism," "The Individual Versus Society," and "Society and Its Faults."

A Reader-Response Approach

A number of our teachers either said specifically or else implied that they relied heavily on a reader-response approach to teaching literature. (I myself used a reader-response approach to literature for years without knowing there was a name for it.) In other words, these teachers believe a text is only black marks on a page until there is a "transaction" with it on the part of a reader (Rosenblatt, 1978). Thus, the reader's response to the work is every bit as important as the writer's creation of it. As Donna Miller put it, "If teachers utilize a reader-response approach with literature, students can 'buy in' to the literature without the didactic approach of the New Criticism, which does little more than teach students that literature is inaccessible unless one has the [academic background] to interpret it for its 'real' meaning. Instead, students need to feel the accessibility of literature as an art form and to realize that they need not be well-educated to understand it."

Because teenage (and perhaps most) readers tend to respond most fully and enthusiastically to characters and situations with which they can relate, a pure reader-response approach to multicultural literature tends to deemphasize cultural differences in favor of similarities. This was indeed the case with some of our teachers; by having a discussion proceed according to students' reactions either to the text in general or to some aspect of it, those aspects to which students could relate were emphasized over those to which they could not.

Others of our teachers used a less "pure" version of reader response, in that there were specific aspects of the texts they wished students to discuss and hence directed discussion into those areas. Within the confines of a given aspect of the text— for example, the concept of arranged marriages—teachers encouraged free-flowing discussion. They did feel free, however, to explain culturally significant aspects of a text when they felt it would enhance student understanding. Some teachers mentioned using students' familiarity with and knowledge of a given culture as resources to clarify and enhance discussion.

Other Approaches

Although thematic and reader-response approaches dominated, a few teachers mentioned other approaches they took in teaching multicultural literature. For example, in addition to doing some units thematically, Dr. Barbara King-Shaver also had her students study the "structure and language of writing to compare how the same literary effects are achieved by writers of various cultures." Western and non-Western authors' choices regarding elements of writing such as diction, organization, imagery, and point of view were closely examined. Sometimes several translations of the same poem were analyzed and discussed. Barbara commented, "The practice of looking carefully at word choice and imagery is good practice for analyzing any poetry."

Very few teachers mentioned structuring units by genre. In the cases where English courses were taught in conjunction with history courses, units tended to be arranged chronologically. One teacher mentioned the "cultural artifact" approach but did not yet know enough about it to attempt it.

Enhancing the Lesson

Most of our teachers spent a good deal of their class time in conversation with their students about the literary works they were studying. However, the teachers also tried in various ways to enhance these conversations, to enliven and enrich them with other kinds of activities. Following, is a sampling of some of the enhancement activities that teachers reported using successfully in their multicultural classrooms.

Journal Writing.   Many of our teachers reported having their students keep journals in which they record their personal responses and reactions to, as well as questions about, the literature they are studying. Donna Miller said, "The primary goal is for students to see their personal responses as a basis for literary interpretation. The opportunity for dialogue with one's own thoughts, provided by these thinkbooks [journals] and generated by a text, can enrich students' understanding of themselves as makers and shapers of meaning." Donna sometimes has her students reflect in their journals on specific questions about concepts like prejudice and superiority. For example, she once asked students "to journal" on the following question: "What if museums, universities, and government agencies could put your dead relatives on display or keep them in boxes to be cut up and otherwise studied for anthropological, biological, or medical reasons?" In addition to being valuable as personal reflections, journal writings often become, according to Barbara King-Shaver, important material for in-class discussion.

Story and Poetry Writing. Based on characters, themes, and issues from works being studied, students write original poetry and fiction. This kind of exercise, in addition to fostering student creativity, helps develop in students a greater understanding of many elements of the literature they are studying, including insights into the way in which different literary works are constructed.

Preparing and Sharing Meals From the Country/Culture Being Studied. This exercise can of course be fun and fulfilling, but it should be educational as well. Gayle Jackson, whose class included Chinese, African American, Caucasian (of many ethnicities and religions, including Mennonite), and Thai students, reported great success with her cultural cooking project. (Students also researched and gave reports on their various cultures—see later discussion.) Although some teachers lightly mocked this activity as stereotypical and milquetoast multiculturalism, proponents noted that good discussions could evolve around questions like what it means that students couldn't find certain needed ingredients in their local Midwestern supermarket for, say, an Indian meal they wanted to prepare for the class.

Students Research Their Own Ethnic/Cultural Backgrounds and Report (in Writing/Orally) on Them to the Class. In many cases, students have surprisingly little knowledge about their own ethnic/cultural backgrounds, although often they know a great deal about the popular or local culture. One of our teachers reported some of her White students as telling her they "had no culture." An assignment such as this opens the door to aspects of students' lives about which they may not have even previously thought. Other students are deeply knowledgeable about and proud of their heritages, and are only too glad to be given the opportunity to share them with their classmates. The research can include interviewing relatives, friends, neighbors, merchants, and elected officials; looking for old photographs, recordings, and films; as well as reading whatever relevant materials they can find around their own homes, in the library, and perhaps for those fortunate enough to have access to computers and modems, even on the internet.

Students Make Family Trees. This opens another door to understanding and appreciation of one's ethnicity, culture, and family. Because the assignment involves the study of one's own flesh and blood, history comes alive.

Ethnic Writers/Storytellers/Historians/Performers and So On, Address Students.
Quite a few of our teachers related that multicultural guests—from a Native
American oral historian/storyteller to a Buddhist monk to a troupe that performed
African folktales wearing authentic African garb—provided an important enhance-
ment to their study of multicultural literature (see also "Providing Background
Information" discussed previously).

Students View Films.   Some of the films teachers have shown parts or all of to
their students include: *I'll Fly Away, Mississippi Burning, El Norte, Raisin in the Sun,
Learning Tree,* and *Power of One.* Gayle Jackson sometimes uses older films and
television shows to demonstrate to students how stereotypes were perpetuated:
"Blacks were always on the short end of the stick . . . always depicted negatively;
they always [played] roles that made [them] ashamed of their own background."

Others.   One teacher, Donna Miller, had students perform a Navajo naming
ceremony in order to help students understand the significance of names in Navajo
culture. Another teacher had students read Coyote stories aloud. One class made
masks. Several teachers had their students act out scenes from the literature they
were studying. Some teachers had students listen to or actually play instruments
from various countries/cultures. Students have made posters of countries from
which the literature they were studying derived. One teacher had students read and
discuss aphorisms derived from different cultures in order to examine how a given
culture's values are embedded in its sayings.

This list of enhancements, although brief, does provide a sense of some of the
creative ways teachers of multicultural literature embellish their classes. If nothing
else, it gives one a strong sense of the possibilities that exist for extending the ways
students can learn about cultures and therefore be more receptive to the literature
of those cultures.

Assessment

By and large, teachers in our study reported assessing their students' work with
multicultural texts in many of the same ways they assess student work with any kind
of text. That is, through tests, which might include short answers but generally focus
on essays (many of our teachers use portfolios and journals for student writing),
through participation in class discussions, and through participation in projects,
which are often, although not exclusively, cooperative projects. (See the "Enhancements" section discussed previously.)

TEACHERS' PERCEPTIONS OF THEIR STUDENTS' REACTIONS TO MULTICULTURAL LITERATURE

Given all their research, planning, and effecting of strategies, how do teachers feel
their students are responding to multicultural literature? Teachers' assessments of
their students' reactions are formed by everything from intuition to student response
journals to overt, sometimes blunt, student feedback in class discussion. (It should

be noted that for a variety of social and psychological reasons, teachers' perceptions may not always accurately reflect their students' own reports of their reactions.) I discuss some of the specific works that teachers report as being successful with students, and some that teachers say simply flopped. I also discuss the potential volatility of classrooms in which sensitive cultural subjects are broached.

Broadly speaking, teachers' reports indicate that students respond to multicultural literature in many of the same ways that they respond to other kinds of literature. That is, among other things, they sometimes like it and are moved or inspired by it, and they sometimes dislike it and are bored or even angered by it. Often, they themselves are not particularly interested in or concerned with "cultural" issues, at least not on an academic or literary level, but rather are interested simply in whether or not they can "relate" to a piece. They also, of course, want to pass the test. Furthermore, in order for students to find characters and situations with which to relate, they have to do the reading first. Although not a focus of this study, lurking not far away from any discussion about high school literature classrooms is the issue of the nonreader. Simply getting students to read anything, according to several of the teachers in our study, is one of the greatest challenges they face.

Literature From Students' Own Cultures

When teachers were asked if their students naturally brought up cultural issues or if they (the teachers) needed to direct students toward cultural issues, most teachers who answered the question reported that students were not inclined to focus on issues of culture unless and until they were guided into a discussion of such issues, and unless the culture was their own. As Donna Miller wrote, "Students don't feel motivated to go beyond the text on their own. Their intellectual curiosity is not powerful enough to be self-initiating." In cases where students were reading works from their own cultures, however, most teachers reported generally positive responses, including greater participation in discussion and more involvement with texts and projects. One teacher, for example, described how a shy, quiet Asian girl, normally disinclined to oral participation raised her hand to point out that a line from a Chinese poem being studied was not particularly well translated. (The students were given a copy of the poem in the original Chinese as well as the English translation.) The student was asked for her translation of the line, and the teacher agreed that it was indeed more poetic and worked better than the originally translated line in terms of its fit with the whole poem.

A teacher whose students were primarily Native Americans reported that she enjoyed having students read pieces that stereotyped Native Americans because those pieces seemed to inflame her students, getting them passionately involved with the piece and with the issue of stereotyping.

Hispanic students, said one teacher, when reading and discussing Anaya's *Bless Me Ultima*, loved the book and "felt somewhat like mini-experts on the cultural legends and the language." Another teacher wrote, "I've seen how interested [minority students] become when someone is reading a story from their culture."

A teacher reported that students felt especially proud when they could report to their parents that they were reading a work from their own culture. "Then, their son or daughter comes in [to the classroom] grinning from ear to ear: 'My parents know that!'"

Overall, many teachers reported that minority students, students of color, and students of various ethnic and religious backgrounds showed pride and increased interest when works from their own cultures or backgrounds were studied. However, teachers also frequently reported that students were extremely defensive about and sensitive to criticisms of their own cultures. In several cases reported to us, passions grew strong and teachers had to impose order on situations where students defending their cultures against student-critics threatened to get out of hand. "They have their prejudices," one teacher said about all of her students.

So, then, what of the reactions of students who were not members of the culture being studied? Reported results were decidedly mixed. For the sake of organization, we discuss these issues in terms of positive and negative reactions.

Positive Student Reactions to the Literature of Other Cultures

When things go well in a multicultural literature class, students come away with opened eyes, a changed perspective, and a new attitude. "Reactions so far have been great," reported Marge Abbott. "I have even been able to dispel many stereotypes." Many teachers reported that they felt their students were coming to understand and appreciate other cultures as a result of reading and discussing their literature.

Recognition of common problems was one key for students in learning to accept people of other cultures. One teacher felt that when her students saw a problem to which they could relate their own lives, they tended "to be interested in how the character(s) solved the problem and what methods or solutions were culturally acceptable to [that] character's society."

Another wrote, "Students often write that they are surprised that other ethnic groups—besides their own—experience prejudice." These discoveries help students "develop understanding and empathy for others," she said.

On the other hand, sometimes what attracted students' interest in the literature of another culture was the culture's radical dissimilarity, at least in some respects, to their own. Several teachers, for example, mentioned the lively discussions that ensued around the issue of arraigned marriages in India. Students of Western European descent generally were appalled at the notion of being "forced" to marry someone. Showing and modeling sensitivity to the feelings of the often-conflicted Indian students was noted by several teachers as of the utmost importance during these discussions.

Sometimes students were profoundly disturbed by their previous ignorance of a cultural issue. After reading and studying a Native American work, Dorothea Susag quoted the reactions of several of her non-Native American students:

"Why aren't the Indians more bitter towards Whites?"
"[I learned] the importance of listening to both sides of the story because one side you may like better, and you will want to believe that side more than the other."
"There is more than one story behind an incident—half the information you are used to believing can be one-sided and the other side of the matter won't be told; to draw a logical conclusion of your own, you are at a loss without all the necessary information."
"I became aware of the amount of understanding we need to use when reading literature that comes from a culture different from our own."

Student reflections were a most useful part of one Barbara King-Shaver's lessons. These reflections indicated that, "[Although] not all students are convinced it is important to study [world/multicultural] literature, the vast majority do see benefits in it." Barbara related to us the results of part of her final exam in which students were asked to write a persuasive essay dealing with the question, "Should multicultural literature be required for all students in public schools in this country?" The results: "14 students argued for multiculturalism/pluralism in the high school literature curriculum, and 6 students argued for assimilation of cultures." Two others, the teacher told us, argued a middle ground: "These were the most unsuccessful papers from a persuasive writing point of view."

Negative Student Reactions to the Literature of Other Cultures

Issues of culture, race, ethnicity, and religion are sensitive and divisive. Most of our teachers, at one time or another, have reported experiencing at least some resistance, be it passive or militant, to the literature of cultures they have attempted to study with their students.

We have already seen that some teachers feel their students come from homes where parents are prejudiced against people of certain cultures, ethnicities, or races. We have also seen in several places in this chapter that teachers fight a constant battle against stereotyping. One teacher wrote, "Students see a culture one way and they don't even want to read about it." In the introduction to this chapter, we saw how teachers themselves, for complex reasons, can sometimes perpetuate "silences" about race and class.

Probably the most common negative response to multicultural literature our teachers reported hearing from their students was "Why do we have to learn about. . . ?" Said one teacher, "Students don't see the relevance in learning about other cultures." They tend to be, according to another, "ego and ethno-centric." Said Joyce Greenberg Lott, "Some students are quite vocal about their own ethnicity—or a preferred ethnicity. For example, African American students have complained, 'Why do we have to learn about the Chinese?' even though we had already studied Africa. They said they should have a choice in the culture they studied."

Another teacher attempted to explain the resistance of her non-Native American students to studying Native American literature: "We are close to two Indian reservations and do see much in terms of negative modeling, so students have difficulty seeing beyond that and looking for the beauty. The resentment is strong but not altogether unfounded."

Students exhibit "strong fears when they read and hear ideas which differ from what they have believed," according to one teacher. Perhaps its a kind of self-defense that causes them to mock or otherwise resist learning about different cultures and peoples.

One teacher sounded particularly heartbroken when she wrote about coming to the end of a lesson that had gone well and that she thought had achieved at least, to some extent, her goal of breaking stereotypes and helping students to appreciate cultural differences and to recognize similarities—only to overhear students using the same kind of derogatory and stereotypical language about members of the culture they had just studied that they had used beforehand. Had anything positive been achieved for all the work they'd done together? "The question still haunts me," the teacher wrote.

METAPHORS FOR TEACHING MULTICULTURAL LITERATURE

One of the last things we asked of our teachers was to try to come up with metaphors that might describe how they saw themselves as teachers of multicultural literature. Unfortunately, a larger than usual percentage of the teachers did not respond to this request. Perhaps this was so because the request came too near the end of the school year. Perhaps teachers felt they had nothing significant to contribute. There are probably other reasons as well. In any case, because we felt that metaphors presented yet another important window into the world of multicultural literature teaching and learning, we searched through the teachers' writings and pulled out some of the metaphors they used in describing their own and their students' roles as teachers and as participants in the study of multicultural literature.

In many cases teachers saw their roles and their students' roles as more similar than different. They were uncomfortable with some of the traditional models of teachers as purveyors of information and knowledge, and of students as passive recipients. It was not at all uncommon for them to write lines like "We're all discovering these things together." In most cases, therefore, the metaphors listed next easily apply to both teachers and students.

Metaphor: Guiding/Searching/Excavating/Exploring/Cartography. "We are looking for evidence"; "finding material"; "discovering new and relevant pieces of literature"; "Arguing in class discussion is part of the territory"; "We have a lot to cover"; "We're on the road to finding we are one people"; "I lead them into strange lands and then give them the opportunity to explore each area in depth."

Metaphor: Connecting/Building Bridges. "Students are pleased to see the human connection . . ."; "Humanity links us all"; "We look for cross-cultural links"; "[Multicultural literature] can bridge prejudicial gaps."

Metaphor: Seeing/Hearing/Touching. "We look at culture through our eyes!"; "Teachers lack clarity about what culture is"; "Students interpreted [literary works] according to their own views"; "voices of ethnic groups"; "We can understand another culture and also reach for our own"; "The greatest opportunity is to reach the student of another culture."

Metaphor: Virtual Reality. "If literature can become a virtual reality experience . . . it can be meaningful and exciting and personal to students."

Metaphor: Chef. "I see myself as a chef. A chef who seeks new, exciting recipes to present to his patrons in a manner that makes their eyes light up (or at least sparkle) and perhaps ask, 'What is this?' And hopefully, 'May I have some more?' I may be different from other chefs since I encourage my patrons to enter my kitchen and experiment with all the wonderful mixture of ingredients and equipment that can lead to all kinds of discoveries. Finally, we share our concoctions with one another. Some we like, some we don't, but we enjoy the exploration and learn about ourselves and others."

Searching, exploring, connecting, touching, tasting—what emerges most saliently from this admittedly small but powerful compilation of metaphors is a sense of the intense commitment on the part of these teachers to sharing their passion for and belief in the importance and richness of the literature they teach. They clearly love the ground of literature upon which they tread, even when it is new and unfamiliar territory, and they clearly want their students to love it, too. Such passion is contagious and inspiring.

DISCUSSION AND IMPLICATIONS

The use of multicultural literature in high school English and language arts classrooms is helping some students come to a better understanding of the "other," and in some cases at least to see that—behind the accent or the skin color, the dress or the customs—the other is not so different after all. It is helping other students to realize just how different the "other" can be, but that that difference can, ideally, contribute to the "rainbow" or the "tapestry" or the "gorgeous mosaic" of the greater society. Furthermore, it is helping some traditionally marginalized students to feel that they belong. Multicultural literature, perhaps in a modest way, is contributing to the mending of some of society's cultural problems.

On the other hand, the study of multicultural literature in the classroom is causing some students to feel, because of their accidental "majority" status, that they are guilty, or that they are "on the way out," or that, as one teacher reported many of her white students telling her, that "they have no culture." Some minority students insist on "equal" time for their cultures, even when time doesn't permit equal treatment of all literary works. Some students want to be able to choose the cultures they study. Prejudices, stereotypes, fears—all of these can emerge in discussions in the literature classroom, and emerge with a vengeance. Teachers must be prepared and able to deal with the volatility that a discussion of issues of culture can and does produce. Multicultural literature, clearly, is causing some problems.

But the focus of this chapter has been on teachers, and so should be the concluding words. The vast majority of teachers in this study, despite the problems they have encountered along the way and reported to us with candor and insight, say that they have no intention of turning away from the wealth of new and/or newly discovered literatures they and their students have been exploring (although they may, in fact, be getting tired of the label "multicultural"). If anything, they want more of it. They want to know what else is out there. They want to find and share with their students quality works (as they themselves define quality) from Vietnam and Tibet and Colombia and Montana and Mexico and the South Bronx. One gets the powerful impression from reading their reports and letters, from chatting with them on the phone or via e-mail, and from meeting them in person, that they are voracious, receptive, thoughtful, articulate, passionate, discriminating read-ers—ideal readers—multicultural bibliophiles. What's more, they bring these quali-ties into their classrooms, which makes them pretty darn good teachers, too.

The question of who determines what literature is to be considered "quality" literature is one we do not delve into in this chapter, beyond stating that we respect the ability of each teacher, in the course of a lifetime of studying and teaching literature, to have developed and continue to develop his or her own personal criteria for what qualifies as quality literature. Myrna Steele said, "There are qualities of good literature that have been established, and I don't question those standards. I respect the standards that have been established long before I was born. All literature that I choose is based upon those standards." Stacie Valdez made the following point about standards for judging multicultural literature: "Of course this literature has to be judged according to the same standards as traditional literature, otherwise it becomes . . . tokenism. I have to be able to justify it according to same literary standards as I justify Dickens and Shakespeare."

That stated, we acknowledge that a complex of forces, including political, social, economic, and spiritual ones, all contribute to the ways in which individuals read, reason, and see.

5

A Theoretical and Practical Conclusion

❧ ◆ ❧

José Meléndez

The studies presented in the preceding chapters offer us glimpses of what might be occurring in classrooms as teachers and students attempt to engage other cultures through their literatures. The picture is a complex one. Teachers, for their part, report a mixture of goals for teaching literature from other cultures, which although not mutually exclusive may seem at times contradictory. They speak about teaching to appreciate differences and similarities among cultures. They speak about sensitizing students to stereotyping at the same time that they search for texts that "represent cultures." They also outline the difficulties encountered in their endeavors. Foremost among these are the ambiguity and confusion about notions of culture, unfamiliarity with other cultures, lack of certainty about which texts are better at granting access to a culture, and student resistance to shedding stereotypes and engaging in the cultures of others. Teachers also report encouraging success stories. They express enthusiasm at having found literature of high aesthetic quality that is also culturally informative. They describe instances of students' heightened awareness of cultural nuances, differences, and similarities.

The studies involving students also add to the complexity of the picture. On the one hand, Jordan (chapter 2, this volume) reports that her subjects were often not aware that the text can be a cultural artifact, and many even reacted negatively to the idea of reading about peoples from other cultures. These students did not consciously consider questions about culture to be of primary importance given that the questions have been muted or absent in their school experience of literature. At the same time, the students made use (and sometimes misuse) of available information on the backgrounds and histories of authors and texts and seemed to react to some cultural differences, similarities, and nuances they perceived through their readings. Some were aware of their cultural backgrounds, which they tended to individualize. Some were not, especially those from "White" or "Anglo" ethnic backgrounds.

Cruz and Meléndez (chapter 3, this volume), on the other hand, report that their subjects were aware of the cultural dimensions of literature texts. All subjects were aware of their cultural backgrounds although some expressed this in more ways than others. They required information on authors' cultures and readings, and recommended that these be included in the study of literature.

These findings are contradictory but do not necessarily cancel each other out. It is possible that notions of culture are part of the background knowledge of most students, but that they do not use it in their reading of literature if they have learned to focus on other things. The school encourages references to the literal understanding of the texts, its broad thematic ramifications, and the personal reaction of the individual students. In many classrooms there may be little call to bring cultural knowledge to bear on literature reading. This could explain, in part, Jordan's findings. She administered questionnaires to secondary school students in classrooms. Cruz and Meléndez used a combination of one-on-one interviews and individualized readings in an informal, out-of-classroom, setting. Their subjects were college-bound students of Dominican and Puerto Rican background. These two studies suggest that the contexts in which the reading takes place—the reading situation—and the students' cultural backgrounds are important factors to consider when examining the cultural dimensions of literature reading.

The complexities and contradictions glimpsed through the studies in this volume are not exclusive to classrooms; they reflect the larger picture of a society that is coming to grips with its own cultural diversity. As classrooms themselves become more diverse they turn into places where cultures meet to converse or be silenced. To understand the nature of these issues, and what they imply for teachers and students of literature, it may be a good idea to step back for a moment and briefly examine this larger social picture and its links with education. It is easier to speak about what culture means, and how to combine its study with that of literature, if we do this first.

THE LARGER PICTURE

The connection of literature education and the study of culture does not exist in a vacuum; it is intricately linked to the growth and multiplication of ethnic and other interest groups in the United States—a situation common to most major nation states in our world. There is a claim from many of these groups to make their histories and cultures legitimate curricular domains. As the teachers in our study demonstrated, a good number of educators second this claim, and believe in the educational value of studying the cultures and histories that compose our society. In fact, many educational systems have incorporated into their curricula language supporting multicultural education. There are other groups and educators that do not consider these attentions to cultural diversity legitimate or important. In their view, the time and effort dedicated to the study of cultures is a distraction and dilutes the energies and resources needed for teaching mainstream cultural literacy. The tensions and dilemmas that accompany the coexistence of many cultures are part of these debates concerning approaches to cultural education, and have found their way into deliberations about the literature curriculum.

The stakes seem truly high. Democratic societies in which diverse groups coexist face "a pluralist dilemma." This phrase, coined by Brian Bullivant (in Lynch, 1986), refers to the dual pull toward social cohesion and cultural diversity that these societies experience. If the forces of social cohesion are allowed to override all others, the result could be assimilation. This could weaken the vitality of the cultures in a society and move its groups closer to a uniformity in which society members lose their self-identity and heritage. A great deal of cultural richness could be lost as we become more standardized. On the other hand, some fear that unrestrained diversity can lead to social strife, and even apartheid, as dominant groups impose their interests by force or as cultural chasms become insurmountable. Either outcome necessitates more than mere cultural pluralism for its manifestation. Other economic and sociopolitical forces have equal and perhaps stronger influence in the processes alluded to by Bullivant in his "pluralist dilemma" scenario. However, the fears, apprehensions, dreams, and hopes that find their way into the debates are real enough in the minds and souls of those involved in these debates. This alone makes the exploration of the alternatives a worthy task.

SOCIAL COHESION AND CULTURAL DIVERSITY: FACING THE ALTERNATIVES

At various moments in their histories, most societies have opted for assimilation. This usually happens at the beginning of massive processes of nationalism or at times of large-scale immigration. United States society at the turn of the century, and England and Australia in the late 1950s and early 1960s, are examples of the latter. Indonesia and some of the sub-Saharan African countries doing away with tribalism at the time of their independence exemplify the former. There have been also instances of social division along ethnic boundaries, such as the former South African apartheid system, the former Yugoslavia, or the alienation of the Palestinian Arabs inside Israel. In such circumstances of social division along ethnic boundaries, both societies are committed to serious political measures to cope with these circumstances. In fact, it is common for present-day societies to attempt some form of synthesis between cohesion and diversity. One way to attain this synthesis is through integration. Integration recognizes everyone's right to equal opportunity and participation, with the expectation that some form of social and cultural fusion will emerge. Another option to the pluralist dilemma is to accept and promote cultural pluralism within an atmosphere of social consensus. This formula also advances equality of opportunity and participation, while also encouraging groups to retain their cultural and ethnic allegiances. At the same time, they are expected to share common values, beliefs, attitudes, and behaviors with the rest of society.

Although very seldom attempted, there are models that take the premise that relationships among social groups also involve an element of conflict. These approaches uphold cultural diversity, but include some form of conflict negotiation and resolution as part of the dynamics of social coexistence. Current policy in Eritrea is a case in point: There is a deliberate attempt for all groups to remain separate but at the same time to enforce cooperation on national issues. In general, the goals of social cohesion and cultural diversity exist as opposites between which social and educational policies fluctuate; and "policies tending to either polarity are usually legitimated by reference to one of the common values of . . . societies such as equality and freedom" (Lynch, 1986, p. 4). Proposals for teaching culture and literature also fluctuate between these opposing polarities.

How do these tendencies take shape and begin to influence policy? Yehuda Amir (1992) examined the way these processes have played themselves out in Israeli society. He suggested that "The path a society chooses will to a large extent depend on the needs, beliefs, attitudes, and behavior of the majority group which has at its disposal the power and ability to direct and control society according to its own preferences" (p. 25). Stemming from this perspective, Amir suggested assimilation or separatism as the only alternatives to diversity. However, these are not the only alternatives. Perhaps the idea that the interests of majorities (or, for that matter, the elite) determine social outcomes is too inflexible and mechanic. This may be the general direction that events take in society, but social processes are a bit more complex than that. Deterministic theories cannot explain the emergence of the other alternatives to the "pluralist dilemma," such as integration, pluralism, and conflict negotiation, as suggested previously.

FROM MYTH TO METAPHOR:
MAKING THE CONNECTION WITH EDUCATION

In Australia, Millicent Poole and Judith Sachs (1992) introduced the notion of myth to describe these social dynamics and how they work. A myth is not a falsity or an illusion; rather, it functions as "a way of structuring and ordering reality, . . . the unquestioned taken for granted assumptions individuals use to operate in the world" (pp. 43–44). Individuals and social groups use these myths to express their interests and perceptions in order to channel them into action.

Some of these myths are used to promote the agendas of socioeconomically dominant groups. Poole and Sachs called these "dominant myths." They present as an example the celebration of the Australian Bicentennial which, according to them, perpetuated myths of European preeminence without mentioning the thousands of years of aboriginal presence in the country. Alongside these dominant myths, Poole and Sachs proposed the emergence of alternative or countermyths. These come about as a reaction to dominant myths and become "instrumental in presenting dissenting voices to oppose the dominant myths" (p. 38). In the case of the Bicentennial, for instance, aboriginal groups boycotted the official celebrations or held their own. In general, organized pressure groups find expression in the popular media and manage to articulate and present countermyths.

Myths are deeply held images or beliefs that operate inside of us at an unconscious level. In this rudimentary form, myths are deemed by many as contradictory, incoherent, and irrational. Unfortunately, much of people's collective behavior based on the myths of a culture does little to disprove these views. However, when we bring them to our attention for careful and critical examination, our myths can be transformed into powerful tools. These can be used as metaphors to explain sociocultural processes and elaborate effective social and educational models, such as integration policies, cultural literacy, and multicultural education.

How exactly can metaphors help us reflect and act on cultural education? James Lynch (1986) presented an account that permits one to see the workings of myth, and could be very helpful for critical reflection of contemporary multicultural societies, although Lynch used the term *ideologies* instead of *myths*. An ideology is less clearly grounded in the cultural memory than is a myth, and is perhaps more malleable, but the two share several features.

Societies have need of ideologies in order to justify and sustain both support for and motivation toward the policies that the state wishes to implement. As Lynch maintained, such ideologies also act as the motivation for individuals and groups for their actions vis-à-vis those policies and are, therefore, of fundamental and practical importance to teachers in their ordinary, everyday, professional lives (Lynch, 1986).

From this premise Lynch elaborated a very sophisticated analysis of the workings of ideologies, and proposed the existence of three broad ideological camps within the United States: economic efficiency, democratic ideal (equality of social, economic, and educational opportunities within existing structures), interdependence by means of negotiation and social discourse.

Each ideology represents alternative clusters of values, ideals, and attitudes to cultural pluralism, and influences four different levels of human existence:

> First the level of values and philosophies; second, the structures of knowledge which are built on and derived from those values and philosophies; third, the human social structures which are tailored to fit those structures of knowledge; and last, the control mechanisms which lock the values, structures of knowledge and social organization into a coherent system. (Lynch, 1986, p. 8)

By combining these general ideological perspectives with their levels of influence, Lynch developed a typology of policy options for responses to cultural pluralism (Table 5.1).

With this typology, it is possible to describe the shifts, complexities, and contradictions in social and educational policy in greater detail and flexibility. One may go beyond conceiving changes and contradictions as just separate events occurring one after another; one may explain how—within the same society and sometimes within an single policy—economic, democratic, and even interdependent ideologies can coexist and/or recur. For instance, curricular emphasis on a dominant culture, in the face of diversity, can be interpreted, in part, as a structure of knowledge derived from elitist or instrumental values based on an ideology of economic efficiency. This can be used to describe certain aspects of assimilationist extremism. On the other hand, a stress on a dominant culture can also be associated with egalitarian values. Many integration and affirmative action policies aim at access to a dominant culture based on these ideologies. For instance, transitional bilingual education in the United States incorporates equality values (equal educational opportunity through language provisions) with economic efficiency (e.g., mainstreaming in three years).

More important, the analysis of ideology can help us examine our own myths. In Lynch's own words: "The implications for teachers are that all teachers must scrutinize their own curricula and activities including the organizational patterns and structures within which they work, to lay bare and expose the real underlying value positions inherent within their current activities and professional aims" (1986, p. 10).

TABLE 5.1

Typology of Policy Alternatives for Responding to Cultural Diversity*

| Dimensions | Ideologies | | |
	Economic	Democratic	Interdependent
Value Systems	Elitist Technocratic/ Instrumentalist Stratification Market-oriented	Equal opportunity Individualistic Partisanship Traditionalist	Communitarian Dialectic Intersubjective Emancipatory
Knowledge Structures	Mainstream Culture Monolingual Literacy: -Pragmatist/Vocational Curriculum: Divided by subjects	Student-oriented Mother tongue Multidisciplinary Change by aggregations False democracy	Paradigm shift Multilingual/ Community-oriented Interdisciplinary Global
Social Structures	Economic alliances Socioeconomic groups stratified Traditional roles promoted	Social Cohesion Homogeneity and Equality Traditional- evolutionary: roles earned	Multiculturalism Organic division/ Equity Human Rights Evolutionary- Revoltionary: Roles changed
Social Controls	Economic imperatives Material rewards and sanctions (coercive) Bureaucratic Multinational	Formal participation Subjective auto-control Representative democracy National	Community rules Formal participation Negotiation Local control International

*Adapted from Lynch, 1991.

Teachers must also understand that the students with whom they work will have also received the same type of multiple ideological influences directly or via their parents. As members of a pluricultural society, all of us come into contact with a variety of influences from the different "groups, individuals, and broader social and cultural pressures" (Lynch, 1986, p. 10). This may help explain the contradictory positions of the students, and some of the frustrations of teachers who participated in the studies reported in the preceding chapters.

METAPHORS OF PLURALIST CONSENSUS: JAMES BANKS' WORK

Approaches to cultural diversity in education can be subjected to the same ideological scrutiny. Consensus versions of cultural pluralism also appeal to democratic egalitarian values that inspired racial integration policies in the past. This time, equal opportunity is sought by affirming a group's cultural and ethnic idiosyncrasies while encouraging it to participate in society's "core" values, beliefs, attitudes, and behaviors. The consensus ideology has facilitated important advances in social initiatives, especially in the area of multicultural education, where the celebration of diversity has become an orthodoxy of sorts. In his classification of multicultural education approaches, James Banks (1993a, 1993b, 1994) related this orthodoxy to the contributions and additive levels of the multicultural curriculum. These add "ethnic content . . . to the mainstream core curriculum without changing its basic assumptions, nature and structure" (Banks, 1993b, p. 203). The contributions approach includes separate cultural elements, such as heroes, holidays, and disconnected historical events. Some call this the "three Fs" curriculum (facts, faces, and fiestas). The *additive* approach incorporates multicultural content, concepts, themes, and perspectives interpreted from a mainstream point of view. These two approaches are compatible with one of the most popular metaphors of the pluralist consensus: the salad bowl. In it, cultures are seen as a happy bunch of vegetables tossed together in a sort of culinary peaceful coexistence. It is similar to the bazaar metaphor for multicultural literature instruction described in chapter 1 in this volume.

Banks (1981) developed the notion of consensus beyond metaphors of separate ethnicities coexisting in society without affecting each other. In his book *Education in the 80s: Multiethnic Education,* he used the concept of multiple acculturation together with the metaphor of an "universal American culture" to describe what he saw as actually happening in U.S. society. According to this view, "ethnic groups do not live in tight ethnic boundaries excluding participation within an universal American culture" (1981, p. 16); instead, Banks maintained that they come into contact and influence one another. This is what he meant by *multiple acculturation.* This interinfluence produces the core or universal American culture. At the same time, the different groups retain some of their exclusive ethnic and cultural traits. Later Banks referred to the universal American culture as "macroculture" and used the term *microcultures* for the particular traits that each group retains. Multicultural studies, Banks argued, should include the examination of each group's cultural and historic experiences; the way their interactions have evolved into a macroculture; and how each group interprets and appropriates the values, beliefs, and attitudes of this core culture. To accomplish this, Banks introduced the *transformation* approach to multicultural education. In it, "The structure of the curriculum is changed to enable students to view concepts, issues, events, and themes form the perspective of diverse ethnic groups" (1993, p. 199). As is seen in the following discussion, both the concepts of multiple acculturation and transformational multicultural education can lead beyond consensus ideologies.

THE CRITIQUE OF CONSENSUS

Critics such as Robin Grinter (1992) and Sonia Nieto (1992) observed that most consensus versions of multiculturalism fail to address key structural factors in society that impede effective pluralism. These factors are at the core of racism and discrimination. Such critics do not think that racial and cultural intolerance are merely the result of misunderstanding and ignorance that leave individuals open to racist misrepresentations of non-White ways of life and value systems; these observers indicate that racism is based on learned attitudes of White superiority that help ensure that people both accept as natural the unequal distribution of power and resources between groups, and do not question the social factors that maintain this inequality (Grinter, 1992). Some of these factors are the living conditions of many of these groups, unequal access to employment and services, poor-quality education resulting from tracking and ability grouping, and cultural and linguistic mismatch between home and school (Nieto, 1992).

The very historical roots of multiculturalism are not evident to the consensus approach. Usually, multiculturalism is said to be an outcome of migration or nationalism morphed into an amalgamated state. However, the fact that migration, and thus multicultural societies, are often the product of conquest, war, slavery, and labor exploitation is frequently downplayed or simply overlooked. These originating forces connect directly to the objective conditions of many ethnic groups in advanced industrial societies. Most consensus approaches do not include a conceptual framework to account for these processes and their impact on the multicultural situation.

FROM CONSENSUS TO CONFLICT NEGOTIATION: BANKS' PROPOSALS FOR CURRICULAR AND SCHOOL REFORM

Although James Banks' construct of a universal American culture retains notions of consensus, his proposals for curricular and school reform point in the direction of major structural changes in education. Banks shows a sensitivity to the discrepancies and inequalities that are at the root of the need for change. We have seen previously how the transformation approach is geared to "help students understand concepts, events, and people from diverse ethnic and cultural perspectives" (Banks, 1994, p. 26), but this approach can go beyond that, because it allows students to perceive knowledge as a product of social forces. Banks gave the example of a history unit about the "Westward Movement." In his words (Banks, 1994), this is an Eurocentric way of depicting and organizing knowledge about the encounter of White settlers and the Lakota Sioux in the 19th century. The Lakota were not the ones moving West; they considered their homeland the center of the universe. If one discusses with students the situation of the Sioux and asks them to envision ways in which the Lakota Sioux perspective could depict knowledge about this encounter, students may use phrases such as "the invasion from beyond," "The age of doom," and the like. If students are then asked to propose a more encompassing title for the unit, they may come up with something like "The Meeting (or the Clash) of Two Cultures" (Banks, 1994).

Curricular changes can go beyond the transformation approach. Banks (1993, 1994) proposed a fourth category: the *decision-making and social action approach*. This includes all the elements of the transformation approach, but in this approach students make decisions on important social issues and take action to help solve them. Banks included the following components in this approach (in Banks, 1993, pp. 205–206):

1. A decision problem or question (i.e., What actions should be taken to reduce prejudice and discrimination in our school?).

2. An inquiry that provides data related to the decision problem. Examples of questions are: What is prejudice? What is discrimination? What causes prejudice? What are examples of prejudice and discrimination in our nation, community, and school? Banks suggested that this inquiry be interdisciplinary and include readings from the various social sciences, biography, fiction, poetry, and drama.

3. Value inquiry and moral analysis. Students are given opportunities to examine, clarify, and reflect on their values, attitudes, beliefs, and feelings related to racial prejudice and discrimination. Case studies taken from newspaper and magazines are used to involve students in discussion. Banks also mentioned the pertinence of literature from minority groups for case study analysis.

4. Decision making and social action. Students make reflective decisions about the issues studied, based on results from the second and third components of this list. By synthesizing knowledge and values they may determine what actions, if any, to take, such as writing a letter to a local newspaper suggesting ways that treatment of ethnic groups in the newspaper can be improved, working to improve racial relations in the school, and so on.

There are good reasons to expect that by focusing on the structural aspects of problems such as racism and discrimination, and by being allowed to direct their energies into concrete actions to confront these problems, teachers and students can go beyond dynamics of guilt and blame and into more constructive ways of facing these issues. Banks conceded that the transition from a mainstream to a social action curriculum does not occur overnight. He suggested a "mixing and blending of approaches" (1993, p. 207) to effect the transition or, at least, bring about some of the benefits of a multicultural curriculum.

Banks (1993) recognized that, to be far-reaching, these type of curricular changes require a major restructuring of schools. This means "a fundamental examination of the goals values, and purposes of schools and a reconstruction of them" (Banks, 1994, p. 37) This proposition implies that "the total system is recognized as the problem and is the target of reform" (p. 37). According to Banks, this is necessary because current school practices and arrangements show very little success with minority students for many reasons, including negative perceptions and low expectations. Advocating school restructuring, curricular transformation, and social action approaches moves Banks' proposals from the consensus into the conflict negotiation arena. Even if his paradigm of a universal American culture is basically consensus-oriented, these proposals are bound to meet resistance in many contexts, as Banks himself recognized. But perhaps it is not necessary to abandon the universal American culture metaphor to accommodate Banks' proposals for transformation and reform.

THE UNIVERSAL AMERICAN CULTURE: AN INTERPLAY OF UNITY, HETEROGENEITY, AND DISCREPANCY

The conflict and contestation approaches to multiculturalism lack metaphorical images beyond themselves. This is perhaps symptomatic of a tendency in these analyses to concentrate more on examining and describing the causes and impact of structural inequalities and less on exploring alternatives to them. It may be possible, however, to integrate the perspective offered by these analyses with the models and approaches to cultural education offered by Banks and others.

What are good metaphors to help articulate these lines of research and action? In his studies of literary criticism, culture, and empire, Edward Said (1993) introduced the notion of "discrepant experiences" to explore the joint cultural and historical experiences of advanced and developing societies within the context of imperialism. In his view, cultures are not one-sided things untouched by external elements; they are hybrid entities that partake of many often-contradictory experiences and domains and "assume more foreign elements, differences, and alterities than they consciously exclude" (Said, 1993, p. 15). For instance, something as American as the federalist system could be partially traced back not only to the British parliamentary system, but also to the political relations developed within the Iroquois League.

Said's image is compatible with the constructs of dialogism and heteroglossia that Mikhail Bakhtin (1994) developed in his study of discourse in the novel. Bakhtin used these notions to analyze and describe artistic language, but his work also impinged on the social, ideological, and cultural dimensions of language. Thus, the notions of heteroglossia and dialogism are relevant to the study of culture. According to Bakhtin, *heteroglossia* implies that the verbal-ideological world (language, cultural meanings and objects, etc.) is the arena for colliding centrifugal and centripetal forces. Centrifugal forces tend toward uniformity and standardization, fueling the tendencies to assimilation. Centripetal forces tend toward decentralization and diversification. By virtue of these forces, concepts such as ideals, values, and other sociocultural constructions acquire a multiplicity of signification as different generations and social groups appropriate them. Think of the student described in chapter 3 who described himself as 100% Dominican but chose to be interviewed in English and expressed an urban-American dislike for "double talk." This is a picture of heteroglossia in the flesh.

The varied meanings or voices in heteroglossia have the potential of conditioning each other. They enter into our utterances and consciousness with the full import of multivoicedness because each of us belong to different groups and has been subject to varying social influences. *Dialogism* is the process through which these meanings condition each other or prevail over each other. At the same time, societies (usually through dominant ideologies) attempt to bring uniformity to this process of multivoicedness. Heteroglossia means that decentralization and discrepancy, as well as the force of unity, are at the core of cultural life, and not at the periphery where minorities are supposed to exist.

A development of Banks' concept of macroculture can be attempted here using the images of Said and Bakhtin. This would permit incorporation of the general and shared aspects of macroculture—ideals and values of civility, democracy, and equality—that lead to visions of consensus, and at the same time acknowledge and address the heterogeneous, conflicting, and even discrepant aspects of people's shared experiences. Heteroglossia is at work within the very values and ideals of civility and democracy. These can acquire different signification for members of different social groups (women, professionals, ethnicities, etc.). Furthermore, many conditions of a society's common cultural life will create situations not only of diversity but also of discrepancy. For instance, the cultural experiences, habits, and attitudes of many people among White ethnic groups associated with discrimination, racism, and White male superiority have their counterparts in the lives of subordinated groups: frustration; conditions of scarcity; compliant or oppositional behavior; and limited access to employment, resources, and services. These opposite clusters of experiences can be approached as discrepant but interconnected aspects of unified social experience. These experiences are unitary because each aspect cannot exist without the others. They are discrepant because each aspect results in contrasting ways of living these experiences. This interplay of unity, heterogeneity, and discrepancy is perhaps a more accurate way of envisioning a core or common culture. The ways in which heteroglossia and discrepancy are integrated into the macroculture can be explored through a critical-thinking approach to cultural education, an approach offered by Banks.

METAPHORS OF CULTURE AND THE LITERATURE CURRICULUM

The myths and metaphors explored previously influence the way cultural phenomena are studied within the literature curriculum. Therefore, those involved in literature education can also consider Lynch's suggestion to "scrutinize their curricula and activities including the organizational patterns and structures within which they work" (Lynch, 1986, p. 10) to get at the real underlying values of their professional practices and goals.

There are many ways to conceive ideologies about culture and how they affect the study of literature. The trends and ideas presented so far, together with the studies included in this volume, offer a very suggestive set of images. Alan Purves expresses these vividly in chapter 1 of this book. He envisions alternatives to the study of culture in literature, which are described in the following sections.

The Literary Canon as an Art Museum

This is the idea that certain texts are "cultural." Just as when you go to an art museum, or read, for instance, *Macbeth*, *Don Quixote*, or *The Iliad*, you become cultured. The notion underlying this image is that of "high culture," or culture as refinement. Many people view this reduction of culture to refinement as elitist, because they believe it emphasizes individual achievement and subjective cultivation. The assimilationist approach to pluralism adheres to this metaphor, by reducing the canon or overloading it with national writers or authors writing in the "great" tradition. This is the case of those pushing for cultural literacy in the United States. However, this form of assimilation also incorporates democratic or egalitarian values, because it advocates for making accessible to all students works and knowledge formerly reserved for the elite.

Adding a New Wing: The Ethnic Hall

This is the idea that a few selected texts illustrate a culture. Under this tenet, if you read Richard Wright or Langston Hughes you understand African Americans, or if you read Tato Laviera you understand Puerto Ricans. In other words, if you visit the ethnic hall you will get acquainted with the group and know its culture. This metaphor is compatible with the contributions and additive approaches to multicultural education. It is the literature curriculum version of the salad bowl. It is a very good way to begin an exploration of pluralism within literary studies, but teachers should be advised that there are more substantial dishes in the menu. Bear in mind, too, that issues of representation (which texts better portray a culture; which cultures the curriculum should include) are bound to be more pressing if you believe that certain texts grant full access to a culture. The size of the wing becomes important. Remember, also, that this is the ethnic wing; the main exhibits—the mainstream, Greco-Roman, and classic works—are still in the central halls of the museum.

Culture as Accident, or the Bazaar Approach

As expressed by Alan Purves in chapter 1 of this volume, the bazaar approach rests on the idea of universality. This view leads to the conception of cultural differences as accidents or nonessentials. It proposes a fundamental human nature shared by all people across cultures that is basically unchangeable. Purves suggests that this idea is very compatible with the thematic approach to literature—favored by many teachers—which attempts to find connections among peoples. The stress on similarity and connectedness offers a way out of the problems of representation and the superficiality of the contributions and additive approaches to culture. It may also offer a way back to assimilation and ethnocentrism. It is very possible that we project our values and presuppositions as cultural universals, and thus tend to project a theme in our own image rather than induce it from the text and the writer (if such is indeed possible). Because themes are usually imposed on texts by readers, there is always the risk of inadvertently coloring our views about literary themes and portrayals of the human condition in another group's literature with interpretations based on our own cultural presuppositions. We may, for instance, see a struggle for individualism in a work written within a culture where individuals' proper roles should be as subordinate to the group. Thus, we may consider a child in an Asian story as noble when people in that culture view it as disobedient. Besides, cultural differences are potent enough to impact on human sense and experience, which are the stuff of literature. Ignoring distinctiveness may cut access to a great deal of content in the experience of literature.

The Literature Reader; Alias the "Young Anthropologist"

Contrary to the universalistic notions, this approach aims at capturing the complexity and variety in human experience expressed in the literature of different cultures. It deliberately avoids the traps of the contributions approaches. Here, the student of literature approaches texts as cultural documents. Texts do not represent cultures, but they are created in the contexts of cultures. In their works, authors express cultural preoccupation and experiences of their times—the spirit and general feelings of the epoch. In fact, authors and texts participate in the general gestation processes of their cultures and times. In this sense, the reader accepts that any text grants access to a culture, although the scenario is more modest than the ones envisioned in the ethnic hall or the bazaar. The access is limited by each author's perspective and talent, and also by the reader's lack of knowledge or his or her ethnocentrism. Authors say more and less than they intended, and their work is an amalgam of those experiences and topics they chose to write about, their points of view, the means at their disposal, and their creative energies. From this perspective, all literatures are equally valid. All have their geniuses, their clever commentators, and their share of failure and mediocrity. Both the recognition of equality of value and the attempt to enter the writer's world are compatible with the transformational approach to the study of culture. By accepting and validating the multiplicity of perspectives that lie not only among different literatures of the world, but among different literatures of any country or group, this approach opens itself to the experience of heterogeneity and discrepancy that lies at the core of any organized form of human coexistence. However, it requires an act of self-abnegation on the part of the reader.

The Literature Reader as a Cultural Being

This perspective extends pertinent elements of the young anthropologist metaphor to the act of reading. It is, therefore, compatible with the previous account (however, this does not mean that the connection is always made). Here is the idea that reading itself is culturally determined. That is, our epoch, our context, and our experience determine the act of reading in culturally specific ways that are analogous to those processes that interact with the act of writing. Reading thus becomes a creative act. The connections of this metaphor with tenets of reader response and aesthetic theories are unavoidable. They are more thoroughly examined later in this chapter.

Some of the images described here hint to the fact that culture itself appears to be subjected to the mythical processes that were described earlier. That is, people have deeply held and unquestioned beliefs about culture that color their views and actions toward it. Undoubtedly, these very beliefs and notions will determine our outlook on how culture should be studied. Here, too, these images can be transposed to the status of metaphors. Because they influence our practice, it would be a good idea to subject our notions of culture to the same kind of scrutiny. These views are not solely of our invention, a first step could be to acquaint ourselves with their historical, philosophical, and disciplinary origins.

CONCEPTIONS OF CULTURE AS BASIS
FOR METAPHORS

In chapter 4 we noted that several teachers use the terms *confusion, lack of clarity, difficulty,* and *crisis* to describe those situations in which they have had to deal with conceptions of culture and multiculturalism. As the preceding discussion has shown, we cannot simply fault the teachers; lack of training is not the main culprit here. Culture serves so many purposes and has so many meanings that one wonders about the utility of persisting in its use as an intellectual category. When the term *culture* is used in political arguments, its sense remains clouded. Contentions for or against the preservation of other cultures, the defense of national culture, the confounding of culture as taste and culture as an anthropological feature—all become the foci of debate rather than clarifying what is meant by the term *culture.* Much educational parlance equates culture with nationality, ethnicity, quaint and exotic customs, learning modes, and behavioral phenomena. As discussed earlier, many educators also persist on using the term in reference to sophisticated intellectual and artistic products and their appreciation. Anthropology—the discipline that has made the most technical use of the term—registers more than 180 definitions for culture (Klukhohn, cited in Damen, 1987).

This does not mean that educators who wish to grasp whatever it is that lies hidden by the term are misguided. Their desire is fueled by teachers' intuition that the understandings and life experiences they and their students bring to the classroom deeply influence what happens there. Many teachers also know that family, community, race, and other forms of group affiliations permeate these understandings and experiences of life. Somehow culture is, or should be, connected to it all.

Raymond Williams (1977) said that, in medieval times, culture meant "the growth and tending of crops and animals, and by extension the growth and tending of human physical faculties" (p. 11). Studies of culture have come a long way from this idea. However, there is in it a stress on development and activity that is noteworthy, especially when examining later diversification of the concept. Social and political transformations brought about changes in the conception of culture. The idea of "growth and tending of human faculties" was extended to the inner faculties of the intellect, taste, and sensibility as well as their products: scientific and philosophic work, artistic objects, and so on. This lead to a double reduction of the term: *culture* became "high culture," and culture was an individualized manifestation of the subjective mind and its specific works. The notions of refinement and taste through exposure to the classics found in the art museum metaphor of literature studies can be traced back to this development.

The optimism characteristic of the Enlightenment, with its focus on reason and civil society, led people to envision culture and civilization as collective phenomena, the products of rational men making their own history. A great many thinkers, well into the nineteenth century, assumed that civilized men had thought themselves out of a natural state of savagery, from barbarism to civilization in the Western style. The Western ideal of "the man of taste" became something like the endpoint of all cultural evolution—the full blossoming of humanity's psyche. This was the modernist version of the bazaar approach to literature, because these ideas presupposed a "universal" human order. These conceptions resulted in a search for general or universal laws of human intellect and behavior.

Alongside these universalistic interpretations, there emerged other, more relativistic accounts of culture. Johann G. von Herder (1744–1803) took a different view on the ideas of self-development. He accepted their historical relevance, but argued against reducing such complex processes to the evolution of a single and abstract principle: reason. He also rejected that the cultural process was a unilinear advance toward Greco-Roman civilization. In his view, defending the Teutonic culture against the Mediterranean, it was necessary to acknowledge variability and speak about "cultures," not "culture."

Wilheim von Humboldt (1767–1835) took a similar stand in his studies of languages and their relation to cultural phenomena. After doing extensive research on non-Indo-European languages, he noted that different languages and grammars encoded different and particular world views. His lifelong dedication to the study of languages and their world views—or encoded cultures—helped to establish them as valid and worthwhile research domains.

As these ideas gained popularity among the bourgeoisie, many of its members developed a fascination with the foreign and exotic. It became a fad to travel abroad and get a firsthand view of groups and societies from "our possessions" in Africa, Australia, or America. There are some parallels between this dilettante ethnography and the hall metaphor.

Present-day debates about cultural diversity and respect for difference, as opposed to one-sided accounts of a "national" culture, still mirror these other divergent views from the past. In any event, the intellectual developments that took place from the 17th through the 19th century expanded the idea of culture from aesthetic and intellectual achievements to social phenomena. As a result, what slowly came into focus was a view of how, in their interaction among themselves and with their environments, humans collectively elaborate a mechanism of adaptation and response. The products of this mechanism—attitudes, values, behaviors, and even language—were grouped under the umbrella term *culture*.

In North America, anthropologists picked up the lines of inquiry suggested by Herder, von Humboldt, and others. Frank Boas, a European anthropologist who established himself in the United States and helped develop the discipline here, trained his disciples to conduct in-depth field studies on the lives of indigenous groups. Anthropologists started using these field work methods in the United States and abroad. Boas encouraged his students and colleagues to postpone theories about general laws of human thought and culture until enough data had been gathered. As a result, vast amounts of ethnographic data on native groups were collected. The idea was to use these data and infer from them the cultural patterns of the groups studied. Observation was coupled with in-depth probing on cultural meanings as informed by members of the groups under study. From this emphasis on the observable, the material, and the shared emerged a view of culture as transmitted and learned, serving to hold human groups together by providing their members with ways of behaving, adapting, knowing, believing, and evaluating. Readers of literature who wish to get an in-depth feel for the context of a culture through its literary works take a similar stance. These works become artifacts, and their authors informants. Purves used the metaphor of the young anthropologist to underscore the likeness of attitude between these literature readers and Boas' early disciples. Such a set of presuppositions is partially reflected in the comments of some students in our studies when they said they needed more information on authors in order to better understand literary pieces.

20TH CENTURY: FURTHER DEVELOPMENTS
OF THE IDEA OF CULTURE

Anthropology's general description of culture was subject to further developments. In most cases, these resulted from emphases on a specific aspect of the general notions of adaptation, behavior, knowledge, or belief. For instance, some anthropologists associated forms and patterns of culture with a particular group's adaptation to its ecological, economic, and/or social environment. They drew inferences about cultural form and content without recourse to indigenous accounts. It was enough to describe cultures "from the outside" as ways of adapting to the environment.

Other definitions of culture have touched on the cognitive and belief systems—ways of organizing ideas and knowledge. Ward Goodenough is typically portrayed as representing this trend, as this quote demonstrates:

A society's culture consist of whatever it is one has to know or believe in order to operate in a manner acceptable to its members. . . . By this definition . . . culture is not a material phenomenon; it does not consist of things, people, behavior, or emotions. It is rather an organization of these things. It is the forms of things that people have in mind, their models for perceiving, relating and otherwise interpreting them.

The emphasis here is on abstract structures of knowledge and belief that are supposed to exist in the minds of those sharing a culture. This idea evokes Chomsky's notion of linguistic competence supposedly shared by members of a language group (Chomsky, 1976), because it suggests that people within a culture possess a competence component very much like language.

As can be seen, the idea of culture has evolved from an individualistic and elitist notion of refinement to a collective phenomenon, and from a focus limited to Western intellectual and social developments opened to encompass diverse manifestation of other, non-Western populations in their own terms. These later definitions have resulted from ethnographers' work among many different societies, their recorded observations, and informants' accounts. All this work has led to three possibilities for defining culture:

1. The patterns of behavior, belief, attitude, and knowledge particular to a group's way of life.
2. Mechanisms of adaptation to the environment.
3. Cognitive mappings and representations as they exist in the minds of those who share a culture.

These views of 20th century anthropology share a notion of culture as relative to specific groups and environments. The emphasis is on cultural differences. This is not an uncontested notion; among others, Claude Levi-Strauss (1966) proposed the existence of universal traits in the human mind. His studies of general classificatory schemes led in this direction. Universal traits take us back to thematic approaches to the study of culture and literature.

There are those who have tried adopting a synthetic point of view between the universal and the particular. Cross-cultural psychologists such as Harry C. Triandis take this stand. They argue that cultures vary but sometimes it is difficult to say in what way. Their studies aim at establishing true cultural differences, while at the same time testing the generality of psychological laws (Triandis, 1980).

One intuitively senses that culture is at the same time universal, particular, habitual, adaptive, and cognitively constituted. How can such contradictory traits be part of the same thing? Perhaps this is so because they belong to human life—and human life is very complex! This is perhaps why so many people have said so many different and contradictory things about culture. They were looking at a highly complex and contradictory set of phenomena, each focusing on specific aspects of the process, each under the particular assumptions of their own cultural contexts. These assumptions are analytical stances, ways of looking at culture to understand it better. These "ways of looking" should not be confused with what one is attempting to grasp, a practice that has been called *reductionism*. It means limiting the idea of what something is to the few concepts used in a particular analysis. The approaches to culture discussed previously are moments of analysis, not ultimate realities.

Still, the perspectives on culture presented here diverge in fundamental points. Each represents a valid description of culture, but one cannot simply lump them together uncritically as compatible accounts. For instance, if each culture embodies universal traits, cultural differences could be legitimately attributable to differences in degree of progress or sophistication rather than differences in kind. If culture is not a cognitive product but only observable patterns of behaviors, attitudes, and beliefs, there is not much difference between these and habits. If culture is a mechanism of adaptation, then it is environmentally determined; if it is a cognitive mapping, it may be independent of environment.

And how do these differences play themselves out if we consider literature or the other arts? A poem by a Chilean like Pablo Neruda can be seen as part of a grand tradition of poetry, and either standing or falling according to the canons of that tradition. It can be seen as the product of specific environmental forces operating on the poet. It can be seen as having a "Chileanness" that distinguishes it from the works of other Latin American poets. It can be seen as partaking of a universal theme but with a particular Chilean twist. And more, it can throw a reflection on a reader like myself, a Puerto Rican male baby boomer who inhabits a variety of cultural niches—most recently that of a doctoral candidate in an institution in upstate New York.

One does not solve these contradictions by acknowledging that all accounts of culture portray it as shared, interrelated, and learned, even if in fact this is true. What is a good way to work through this complexity and develop some insight that brings together the study of culture and of literature?

CULTURE AND LITERATURE STUDIES

Raymond Williams' analytical stance could help to examine the interplay of culture and literature in a way that is open to multiple and even conflicting interpretations. In *The Long Revolution* (1961), Williams discussed the views of culture examined so far, analyzing the ways in which the study of culture and the study of literature illuminate each other. According to him, there are three general categories of the definition of culture: the ideal, the documentary, and the social. Each category entails a particular methodology for cultural/literary analysis.

The *ideal* proposes absolute and universal values that can be seen to compose a timeless order. To analyze culture is to discover and describe those values in the lives and works of thinkers, scientists, and artists. This timeless order connects with the search for universal themes in literature suggested by some of the teachers in their reports. The *documentary* consists of the body of intellectual and imaginative work that records in detail human thought and experience. Cultural analysis is equal to the criticism of this work of human creation. Such criticism can lean toward the ideal analysis, or it can be historical analysis of given works that are related to the particular traditions, societies, and groups in which they appear. In this last sense, the documentary represents the efforts of those students and teachers assuming an anthropological outlook that enriches their reading by connecting a work to its cultural context. The social offers a description of a particular way of life that expresses certain meanings and values, not only in art and learning, but also in institutions and behavior. This is the focus of anthropological and sociocultural studies.

In literature studies, the social, documentary, and ideal can complement each other. The social analysis corresponds to the search for cultural background information on an author and text. The documentary represents the study of how the culture is envisioned and portrayed by the author in his or her work. The ideal seeks universal elements connecting works both within and across cultures through themes, genres, and motifs.

Williams (1961) proposed that cultural studies should include the "three areas of fact to which the definitions point" (p. 43): general human values and meanings (even if these are not absolute in the idealist sense), the documents that portray general and particular elements of human experience, and the embodiment of such experience and activity in institutions and ways of life. "It seems to me that there is value in each of these kinds of definition, for it certainly seems necessary to look for meanings and values in the record of creative human activity, not only in art and intellectual work but also in institutions and forms of behaviour" (Williams, 1961, p. 42).

A word of caution may be in place here. To posit culture as "values, documents, patterns of behavior, ways of life, networks of meaning" allows us to examine culture in the light of its constitutive elements. This is precisely the goal of the analytical method. However, this could result in an "objectification" of our view of culture, in which we lose from sight the fundamental fact of culture as a lived existential experience. Literature teachers interested in the study of culture face this trap. It can take us back to the "museums and halls" of culture. This can be avoided by keeping in mind that analysis is an initial moment in the study of cultural phenomena.

> It is with the discovery of patterns of a characteristic kind that any useful cultural analysis begins . . . it is with relationships between these patterns . . . that general cultural analysis is concerned . . . but these are recovered in abstraction . . . the most difficult thing to get a hold of is the felt sense of the quality of life in a particular time and place: a sense of the ways in which the particular activities and cultural elements combined into a way of thinking and living. (Williams, 1961, p. 47)

The role that Williams assigned to the study of art and literature is of particular relevance for teachers who want to access the "living culture":

> We can go some way in restoring the outlines of a particular organization of life . . . what Fromm calls the social character or Benedict the pattern of culture . . . possibly however we can gain the sense of a further common element which is the actual experience through which they were lived . . . and I think the fact is that we are most conscious of such contact in the arts of a period. (Williams, 1961, p. 47)

This does not mean that all the members of a society live such experience in the same manner, or that groups share the same culture in the same way. As Said and Bakhtin suggested, a "culture" can and will be comprised of an heterogeneous and even contradictory set of patterns and experiences, because many of its groups and subgroups position themselves at odds within the social arena. Even the general values of ideal analysis will be construed and experimented with differently across groups and individuals. This is also true in the context of international cross-cultural coexistence.

It must be added that the centrality of the category "experience" is a source of debate. Those who think that socially determined knowledge and emotions induce subjective experience consider Williams' position idealist and naive (Hall, 1980). To this charge Williams might assert that such determinism is too mechanistic. Again, the issues are complex and debatable. Nevertheless, just as collectively "lived experience" cannot be adequately understood outside given sociocultural forms of knowledge, attitudes, and emotions, the full import of those structures cannot be fully grasped without some kind of access to the experience through which they are lived.

LITERATURE AND THE COMMUNICABILITY
OF CULTURAL EXPERIENCE

The arts of the various social groups give access to the groups' experiences. They do not exhaust that experience, but the possibility of communication is there. Studies in aesthetic theory and response to literature offer some ideas on how to take advantage of this possibility. The key is to realize that one is dealing with a process of presentation. Art—and literature is by no means an exception—is an act of organization, expression, and presentation of the artist's significant experience that embodies a great deal of "this felt sense of the quality of life of the culture of a society in a given time and place" (Williams, 1964, p. 47) as lived by the artist. Thus, from the artist's point of view an act of internal organization occurs in which the artistic means, the experience being communicated, and the communication itself are effectively elaborated into a work of art. From the point of view of the audience an analogous process can be posited: Perception is also a creative act.

> However successful an artist may have embodied his/her experience it can be received by no other person without the further creative activity of all perception: the information transmitted by the work of art has to be interpreted, described and taken into the organization of the spectator . . . to succeed in art is to convey an experience to others in such a form that the experience is actively recreated . . . by response to the means, actively lived through by those to whom it is offered. (Williams, 1961, p. 34)

The arguments developed in aesthetic theory can help us examine the interplay of culture, text, and reader as well as to realize the educational potential of such interplay.

THE INTERACTION OF CULTURES IN
THE EXPERIENCE OF LITERATURE

One theme that stands out from recent views on literary criticism and aesthetic theory is the unitary nature of all aesthetic experience. No longer is appreciation of art defined as a spectator's disinterested and detached consideration of an "independent" object of art. Arnold Berleant brilliantly captured this idea in his theory of art as engagement: "[A]esthetic engagement then joins perceiver and object into a perceptual unity" (Berleant, 1991. p. 47), but this perceptual unity goes beyond the object and the perceiver. In it, aesthetics of distance give way to a notion of continuity in which the artist, the work, the performer (in art that implies such), and the public fuse in the act of creation. Berleant developed this in his theory of the aesthetic field:

> The concept that best expresses the integral yet complex experience we call aesthetic is the aesthetic field. Here the four factors represented by the object, the perceiver, the creator, and the performer are the central forces at work, affected by social institutions, historical traditions, cultural forms and practices, technological developments in materials and techniques and other such contextual conditions. (1991, p. 49)

The relevance of aesthetic field theory for us is its inclusion of cultural and historic phenomena in the experience of art. According to Berleant, literary criticism has accepted this unitary and culture, inclusive view of art:

> It is one of the discoveries of recent literary criticism . . . that a text does not stand alone. A text requires a cohort of critics and readers, a literary public, a linguistic system, all surrounded by a larger society with its conventions and beliefs, and all placed in an ordered historical perspective to be understood. (1991, p. 105)

The cultures of the reader, the text, and the reading situation are an inseparable matrix, but they are not indistinguishable. Within this matrix, different literary critics give preeminence to either the text and its author, the reader, or the reading situation.

Ingarden (cited in Berleant, 1991) considered the text as the pivot on which the reading experience revolves. Literary works are "integral wholes whose indeterminacies the reader must complete in a 'proper manner' as prescribed by the text" (Berleant, 1991, p. 112). Proponents of mainstream cultural literacy would be very comfortable with this idea, but so would be those who think that a text as artifact gives full access to "its culture."

At the other extreme, Holland emphasized the reader imposing his or her identity and freedom of interpretation in the inkblots of a text (in Dollerup, 1990); a continuous transaction between reader and text occurs in which meaning and feeling are created. Contrary to most literary critics, Holland conceived the contributions of both reader and text as indistinguishable (Berleant, 1991). This proposition agrees with subjectivist notions of reader response, which seem to be the common take on response theory among teachers using this approach. It implies that access to "the other" is improbable. The previous chapter's findings among teachers using response approaches confirm this: "A pure reader response approach . . . tends to deemphasize cultural differences in favor of similarities . . . by having a discussion proceed according to students' reactions either to the text in general or to some aspect of it, those aspects to which the students could relate were emphasized over those to which they could not (Ostrowski, chap. 4, this volume, p. 60). This also supports the claim that approaches overemphasizing similarities risk a regression to assimilation and ethnocentrism, because those aspects "that we can relate to" are bound to be colored by our experiences and cultural perceptions.

Wolfgang Iser assumed an intermediate position: Neither reader nor text can be understood in isolation. In responding to the text, the reader constructs a total situation imaginatively by organizing the intricacies of a text while bringing in past experiences and making it into a personal presence (Berleant, 1991). The text, on the other hand, carries potentials that are realized in the process of reading. These exist in the text in the form of references to social and historical norms, literary works, and social situations or an entire cultural tradition. This highlights the relevance of culture to text, or in Williams' terms, the documentary aspect culture/literary analysis.

Stanley Fish introduced the culture of the reading situation. He also underscored the importance of past experiences. For him, the formal patterns we discern in texts or those we use to interpret them are the product of these experiences. They give meaning to language as we utter, hear, or read it. This does not mean that response is purely individual; it can be verified that readers agree on meanings, interpretations, and judgments. This is so because they belong to interpretive communities that share a body of experiences. These collective experiences, past and present, constitute the culture of the reading situation.

This culture is made of ways of thinking, experiencing, and responding to literature in the course of education and under common social and historical influences (Berleant, 1991).

The culture of the reader and that of the reading community can now be seen as two aspects of the same phenomena. This is nothing new. By definition, culture is a collective entity borne by individuals, but the idea of reading communities allows a clearer reflection on the different cultural contexts that affect the reader's literary experience: home, community, school, society, the epoch, and so on.

HOME AND COMMUNITY

Rearing practices at home and in the community impact on people's reading practices and how the literary experience is approached. Harkness and Super (1993) advanced the idea of the developmental niche to indicate how the general themes, attitudes, and beliefs of groups and their larger societies are transmitted to children in the home and community. This concept could be useful to begin an exploration of how home and community transmit reading practices to children. Three subsystems constitute the developmental niche: the physical and social setting where children live; culturally regulated customs and practices; and the personal sources of those customs and practices, such as parents, siblings, relatives, and friends. These personal sources focus the general beliefs, cultural themes, and attitudes of the group or the larger society into derived and specialized models to handle particular experiences and actions. For example, some middle-class North American parents will take the general theme of independence and develop a specialized model of child/parent detachment. This model will translate into specific practices, such as putting babies to sleep in their own bedrooms, with less frequent protective responses to night crying; allowing for more risk taking; and encouraging self-sufficiency in food intake. Super and Harkness (1993) used the term *ethnotheory* to refer to these specialized models.

Ethnotheories about the uses of language, reading, narrative, and imagery are also developed in the home and community. Shirley Brice Heath (1983) called them "ways with words." These are bound to have a significant influence on how the literary experience is approached. Heath's ethnography in Trackton and Roadville, two Piedmont communities in North Carolina, revealed how each community interpreted and used reading and writing to maintain social relationships, introduce everyday and community-related topics of discussion, gain support for attitudes and beliefs already held—in other words, to maintain the status quo. Both sets of children had difficulty with the idea of school reading and writing, although each group had distinct difficulties. Heath's findings suggest that ethnotheories are not direct adaptations of broader cultural themes to particular circumstances, but instead arise from the particular circumstances that modify those themes.

READING SITUATIONS AND THE CULTURE OF THE CLASSROOM

The classroom community is, to a great extent, a product of the culture of the school. School culture expresses much of its culture in the form of broad curricular principles, such as emphasis on performance, learning as reception (and perhaps critique) of information, skills as discrete, and uniform and measurable behaviors. Classroom interactions and activities can be conceived as a process of socialization in which teachers and students incorporate these general cultural or curricular themes in their personal contacts through the use of special models or ethnotheories.

Much of what is considered literature reading is also subject to interactions guided by ethnotheories adapting these general cultural themes of the curriculum. Classes will be expected to read in order to get the main themes; analyze characterization, imagery, and setting; chart the plot; classify into genre; and so on. Arthur Applebee (1991) verified this in his extensive study of the seven most-used literature anthologies in American schools. (The anthology is a central piece of the curriculum in many classrooms.) Among other things, Applebee examined the cognitive demands of the activities that accompanied the readings in these anthologies. Thirty-two percent of the activities dealt with recall or paraphrasing of information, and 42% with analysis and interpretation. Applebee then examined the anthologized selections. He wanted to ascertain the kinds of content that each selection's activities emphasized. He found that 94% of the selections had questions on character, plot, and setting; 93% on theme or purpose; 88% included questions on language or style (mostly the meaning of words); and 61% on literary themes. As for the study of culture, 31.2% emphasized social or historical background on their supporting activities. However, only 12.9% of selections by non-White authors had supporting activities related to culture or historical background. Figures reported by Applebee in the same study yield an average of only 13.4% for selections from non-White authors across anthologies. The resulting picture is that, on the average, only 1.7% of the selections in the seven most used literary anthologies include activities that probe the cultural background of works by non-White authors. A multicultural approach for a classroom, therefore, must counter the prevailing theme.

Chapter 2 of this volume suggests how past academic experiences, or the cultures of classrooms as interpretive communities, guide students' experiences with literature. The researchers had students place in order of importance the types of questions that should be asked about the literary pieces they read. Overall, students placed comprehension question in first order of importance—an average of 54% across ethnic groups. Questions of culture averaged 18% across ethnic groups. These findings are in keeping with Applebee's figures that show preference for recall, comprehension, and analysis questions over culture questions in literature anthologies. These studies imply that much of the students' focus on "right answers" and text comprehension could be traced back to the value placed by school culture on reading for gaining and understanding information.

Teachers and students, however, have not been all cast from the same mold. Multiple acculturation also happens in classrooms. Based on their personal, home, or community experiences, students and teachers may accept, adapt, contest, or ignore "modes of action" directed by curricular themes. The student survey study also suggests this. The questions students placed in second order of importance still favored comprehension, but there was a slight increase in emphasis on cultural questions across ethnic groups. A detailed analysis of students' responses by ethnic background found that African, Asian, and European American students placed more emphasis on questions about text comprehension. On the other hand, Hispanics and Native Americans favored comprehension and cultural background questions in equal proportions.

Teachers in our surveys showed concerns for the study and experience of cultural diversity, which are not reflected in commercial anthologies or mainstream curricula. These teachers use approaches based on particular and general cultural themes, exploration of difference, and/or the past experiences of students. In other words, the curriculum is not a straight jacket. Classroom personal contacts can be guided by alternative themes and ethnotheories. Groups can and do embark on individual and collective reading in order to explore the world as it is presented in a literary work. They may even be couched into reliving the experiences of the characters or the authors, while making personal and/or collective sense of the work. And again, based on their particular idiosyncrasies, students and teachers may accept, contest, or ignore these alternative practices.

The cultures of the text; the cultures of the classroom, the home, and community (the reading situation); and the reader's take on these (culture of the reader) will interact and shape the nature of the response—the communication of significant experience through literature. The model shown in Fig. 5.1 presents these cultural constituents of the act of literary reading and their interaction.

A note of explanation should help define the terms of this diagram:

- *The text as a cultural document* refers to the social and cultural situations and traditions as the author consciously and/or unconsciously works them into the text (this corresponds to Williams' documentary level of cultural analysis), as well as the author's personal stance and the specific intended contents of the work.
- *The culture of the reader* refers to the reader's acquired ways of approaching the literary text through previous uses of print and encounters with literature. These consist of specific reading behaviors, attitudes, beliefs, and expectations concerning the literary encounter acquired through home, community, and school, as well as overall cognitive modes and styles plus general behaviors, attitudes, beliefs, and expectations acquired through the previously cited sources.
- *The reading situation* is always in the present, and has its sociointeractive patterns guided by specific models of general cultural themes (ethnotheories), and by the ends and means of an interpretive community (e.g., for recreation and pleasure, to satisfy intellectual curiosity, as a class requirement, collective

or individual reading). The reading community may be physically present or may exist subjectively as a frame for interpretation.

- *The literary work* refers to the work as it is constituted in the literary event through the interplay of all of the previous three items.

Like any visual representation, the model that is presented in Fig. 5.1 is static, and we may say of its parts that these are analytic constituents of the act of literary reading but they do not capture the totality of the act of reading and understanding a work of literature. First, as has already been said, in the literary encounter there exists an opportunity to go beyond stated cultural attitudes and beliefs, past behavioral and cognitive modalities, and to apprehend these as they were lived—as existential experience: "to get a hold of the felt sense of the quality of life in a particular time and place" (Williams, 1961, p. 47).

> This experience has sensuous dimensions, it requires somatic involvement; stimulates imaging and imagination, association and the abandonment of memory . . . it can be characterized as a condition: the grasp of a social situation, of a state of mind or a relationship, of the sense of a particular place or a perception of the world, of the very order of things. . . . (Berleant, 1991, pp. 119, 122)

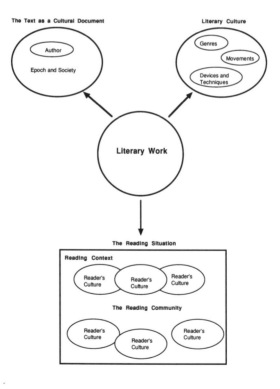

FIG. 5.1. Analysis of the literary event.

Berleant's depiction parallels that of William Anderson's depiction of "biblio-phany," the literary parallel of theophany or epiphany, which is a total enrapture-ment in the reading of a work (Anderson, 1996). Sometimes this possibility is not encouraged; not even from the tenets of response theory. Despite its focus on the reader and the reading situation, much response-oriented criticism still posits that the act of literary reading is predominantly about meaning and interpretation, the main aims of reading in school:

> More recent criticism continues to occupy itself with interpretation, and this centers the discussion of literature around questions of meaning. What has changed is not the function of criticism but its locus, which has now been displaced form the text to the reader . . . formalism, reader response theory, and subjectivism are themselves interpretive strategies: all propose to explain what literature means. . . . (Berleant, 1991, p. 117)

Now if the nature of literary response is the constitution of meaning, interpre-tation, and nothing more, we again risk reducing cultural and aesthetic experience to patterns and things. The meaning that critics seek to explain rests on the experience of literature. It is the account of such an experience, but—as Berleant would say—they invert the order by advancing some theoretical presupposition of what the experience should be and then dictating it. In school literature, an intellectual bias favors cognitive-analytic activity over appreciative engagement or bibliophany. This does not mean that the latter are possible without a basic referential understanding of the language in the page, or that cognitive aspects of the apprehension and organization of literary devices (imagery, rhyme, charac-terization, etc.) are irrelevant, or that readers can be ignorant and mindless about key allusions the author has used. Instead, it means that all of these elements are part of the material that authors and readers use to elaborate the "aesthetic field" in literary experience, but it is the experience that makes literary engagement what it is.

The unitary nature of the aesthetic field as it unfolds in the literary experience is currently captured in Louise Rosenblatt's model of literary transaction. In it, the reader actively creates an *evocation* of the literary work under the guidance of the printed symbols (Rosenblatt, 1994). To this is added response, which is not reduced to cognitive apprehension of meaning but consists of the concurrent stream of feelings, attitudes, and ideas aroused by the work summoned in transaction. Interpretation is a posterior moment in the process, and consists of a reflection on the nature of the *evocation*. Thus, for Rosenblatt, "The aesthetic encounter with literature is a temporal event . . . it is the joining of reader and text in a unified occasion . . . the poem is not an object but an experience . . . it is an event that occurs in the time of experience" (Berleant, 1991, p. 121). Because reader and text contribute equally, it is possible to appreciate how the cultures of texts (the documentary) and readers enter the event, because "The reader brings knowledge, background, personality and the skills of perception and comprehension to activate the ordered symbols of the text" (Berleant, 1991, p. 121).

These considerations move us to propose a some modifications to the earlier model to account for the experiential character of the culture/literary appreciation loci. A more dynamic view is perhaps captured in Fig. 5.2.

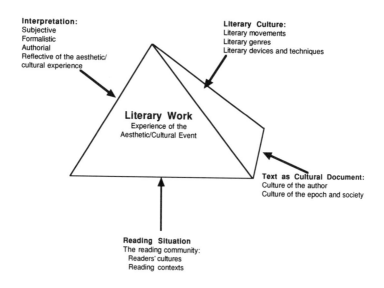

FIG. 5.2.   The literary event as lived experience.

Again, some explanatory notes are in order:

- *The culture of the author as it bears on the text* is the lived personal, social, and cultural situations *as experienced, envisioned, and communicated by the author.* This can be transmitted consciously or unconsciously—it is seen in the documentary level of cultural analysis.
- *The culture of the reader* refers to the reader's way of living, feeling, and understanding the literary encounter based on previous home, community, and school experiences with print and literature.
- *The reading situation* (always in the present) refers to the cultural and socially patterned situation in which literary reading is *lived and experienced,* including such aspects as individual or collective reading; the endeavor of an interpretive community; and the purposes of the community, such as for recreation and pleasure, to satisfy intellectual curiosity, or as a class requirement.
- *The literary work as event* refers to the work as it is *constituted and experienced in the temporal act of response,* through the interplay of all of the previous items.

Although a static picture, the model, we believe, also captures some of the dynamic aspects of the event of literature, and allows for the possibility of bibliophany as well as the more intellectual approach favored in school.

TAKING THE LITERATURE CLASSROOM BEYOND
THE CULTURE TOURS

What does all this mean to those of us who want to integrate the teaching of cultures and literature? Let us accept again that the picture is very complex. Easy step-by-step recipes on how to teach literature and culture is the last thing we need, especially if one wishes to go beyond the culture tour. Still, the previous model can help deepen our insight of the encounter with the literary work, and it is exemplified by many of the practices described in the preceding chapter, some of which encourage an immersion in the text, but most of which represent different intellectual approaches.

Exploring the Cultures of Reading

Perhaps it is best to start here by examining the interplay of the reading situation and the cultures of readers. These are all connected, and a lot can be accomplished there. The first thing to realize is that, in the reading situation of classrooms, teachers and students are dealing with cultural multiplicity at many levels. There is the culture of school as an institution that the curriculum organizes as themes, philosophies, goals, procedures, and so on. There is the culture of the teacher, a composite of training, curricular and institutional expectations, membership in various groups, ethnicity, and the past experiences resulting from all this. Then, there are the cultures of students that are not reducible to their home or ethnic backgrounds. Students also belong to various groups defined by community makeup, ethnicity, schooling, macroculture, nationality, age, and gender. At a personal level, each participant's encounter with literature will be affected by the beliefs, attitudes, knowledge, and experiences resulting from these varied backgrounds. The reading context created by the convergence of these forces and by the atmosphere of the school will also impact on everyone's literary experiences.

Self-exploration and dialogue are good ways in which members of a reading community can gain this knowledge about themselves and their situation. This implies that teachers and students should explore together—through discussion and other forms of encounter, such as gaming or role playing—who they are as readers and members of their various affiliations. Questions to be explored may include: What does it mean for me to be a teacher, woman, man, student, adolescent, child? What does my ethnic background means to me? To you? What are the nature, assumptions, and goals of our literature curriculum? Why should I read literature from a particular ethnicity, nationality, or group? Why should I read literature at all? Why should we, as a group, do these readings? These are some pertinent questions that can be used to open the conversation. *Dialogue* here is meant as exchange of views and ideas, and there is no reason not to do these kind of explorations via the written or electronic word (which students can do individually or in groups). In our research with the Puerto Rican and Dominican students, we began the interviews by asking some of these questions to the subjects. Not only did these questions yield valuable information about the readers, they also helped students to focus their readings aesthetically, culturally, and intellectually.

SELECTING AND CONFRONTING THE CULTURE OF THE TEXT

We found that the issues of most concern for teachers in this respect are (a) what cultures to represent in their choices of texts, (b) which texts better represent a culture, and (c) how to ensure aesthetic quality and cultural representation at the same time.

Choice of Texts and Representation of Cultures

Which cultures are to be represented in teachers' choices of texts? It depends on the reading situation. Perhaps the best approach is to begin with the cultures of the actual students who compose our classes. This opens the possibility for students' intercultural communication and learning. It also communicates a sense of value to the various cultural groups within each classroom. But again, there is value in having students know other cultures. If the class members are up to it, why not involve them in the search for works? This can start with teachers finding the sources and students probing them afterwards. With proper encouragement, students may even be able to find sources themselves. Students interviewed in our study expressed a desire to do such a search.

If one sees fit to go beyond the cultures represented in the classroom, as could be the case with so-called "monocultural" groups, why not start with the national cultures? That is, by virtue of its history, the United States has intertwined its culture with that of other groups and in fact has made these cultures part of its history. Specific historical acts have incorporated Hawaiian Islanders, the Native Americans, the Asian Americans, the African Americans, the Mexican Americans of the Southwest, the Puerto Ricans and other Caribbean islanders, and the various European groups into the culture and history of the country. Therefore, by knowing about these cultures and histories, "mainstream" students are learning about a frequently ignored aspect of their own history and culture.

Texts' Representations of Cultures

As was discussed, cultures are a mix of unitary, heterogeneous, and discrepant patterns and experiences. This means—and this was also pointed out—that no text gives full access to a culture. At the same time, a group's texts are most likely going to reflect this plurality of voices. In other words, the issue of culture representation has to be reconceptualized. More valuable would be to detect works that best present characters, situations, and themes encompassing the multivoicedness and plurality of perspectives present in a culture. In order to understand a group or society better, it may also be productive to select works that represent divergent groups and agendas. Sometimes we are apprehensive of our capacity to do this. We cannot do everything ourselves, but perhaps our students can collaborate with us. The dialogic processes suggested previously may make it possible for students to offer this kind of information about their cultures. In such situations teachers make use of their students as informants. Teachers can also turn students into research assistants when they participate in the search for sources and texts in their cultures. Teachers will know what to do based on the result of the conversations proposed earlier. It is important to talk about these project ideas with student groups before assigning them.

Aesthetic Quality Issues

There is probably "good" and "bad" literature in any culture with a literary tradition, although much that passes by good taste is a matter of subjective judgment. In any event, one does not have to select material that could be mediocre just because it has been written by a someone from a given culture. As a matter of fact, doing this defeats the purpose of cultural education, because one risks taking clichés and stereotypes presented in poorly written texts as the only "representatives" of a culture. Teachers can start by exploring the several comprehensive multicultural anthologies that exist already. On many occasions we will probably need to involve our research skills and visit libraries or other databases.

Aesthetics go beyond taste. If a teacher decides to consider at least some of the ideas exposed in this chapter, then one criterion that can assist in the selection of a text is the text's capacity to provoke an engaged aesthetic experience. This can mean more than finding the work pretty or inspiring; rather, one is looking at its power to activate potent and vivid images of the existential situation of "the other," doing so artistically. Responsive engagement presupposes that talent or power can reside in both the writer and the reader. Thus, the first requirement in searching for the "good" literature in other cultures is an implicit faith in our talent and sensibility, and those of writers and sages of other cultures, to create a literary experience of quality. More than anything else, it is perhaps a matter of allowing ourselves the opportunity to exercise our aesthetic judgment and cultural sensibility.

Understanding the Culture of the Text

"Yes," a teacher will say, "but isn't sensibility culturally determined? And what if I or my students do not understand key allusions and references?" These are very valid considerations. Key allusions and references, together with literary devices, are part of the materials used by authors to create the work of art. And yes, in order to access the text better, it may be necessary to explore key elements of the text's historical and cultural background. Both students and teachers have reported this need in the various parts of our study. But when we question our capacity to understand a work of art, couldn't it be possible that we are assuming that only the informed interpreter can be the proper interpreter? That only the author and those familiar with her or his techniques and ideas can interpret the work? If we believe that the interpretive authority rests exclusively on the text and its creator, then there is no problem with those assumptions, and the matter can be put to rest. If we consider that the text, the author, and the reader are participants in a unified literary event occurring in and across time and space, and if the literary experience is more than interpretation, then considerations of cross-cultural literary apprehension become a bit more complex.

If we give preeminence to what the reader brings to the event, we are left with doubts about the cross-cultural communicability of the experience. There is always a chance that we readers will make the text too much like ourselves. Analogous doubts are possible if the perspective of the writer is emphasized. These doubts lie behind arguments that only women, Africans, Indians, or Hispanics can understand feminist, African, Indian, or Hispanic literature, respectively, because only they share the mentality and experience portrayed by authors of such texts. But if there are elements in the human condition that are accessible to all of us, if we even share some common experiences (albeit many of them from different and perhaps even antagonistic positions), then there is ground for conceiving the possibility for communication. These may understandably sound like big "ifs," but by their very hypothetical nature it does not seem logical to conclude their falsity prior to attempting the experience of cross-cultural reading.

It seems that many of these concerns are a matter of trust; we trust that we can understand "the other" and that "the other" not only wants to be understood but has faith in our capacity to do so. Many good writers in other cultures write not only for people from their own culture but for all humans in general. They want their story to be received and taken into account across cultural boundaries. Readers' understandings of another culture's literary material are deliberately aided by the authors' strategies for deploying familiar and unfamiliar referents and common language in such a way as to facilitate nonindigenous reading (Dasenbrock, 1992).

We can expect, then, that many writers are going to make a sincere effort to communicate. This expectation is shared by many teachers in this study who exhort their students to respect and open themselves to the literature from other cultures. We have seen in their accounts, as well as in students' statements presented in chapters 2 and 3, that this is not always easy or possible to accomplish. It is perhaps never easy. Many times, for instance, students concentrate on simply understanding a story or poem, and do not reflect about other cultural aspects of these texts. But from what we know about cultural phenomena, we can see that this is not necessarily an "acultural" response. Rather, it may be the product of the student's culture as he or she participates in certain school practices, such as reading for information or to obtain a good grade. We are also reminded of the fact that the seven most-used anthologies in American schools include a scant amount of questions about the cultures of non-White anthologized writers. At least we know that once they are made conscious, cultural practices are negotiable, and that it is in our power as teachers and students to make the attempt. Individually, as a dialogic communities and as reading communities encountering texts, we can confront and access "the other." But this does not happen by itself. We have to go get the book, and then open and read it.

Appendix

Summaries of the stories used in the national study:

"Black Hair": A coming-of-age poem by Gary Soto, who is an American of Mexican descent. He is seventeen, a baseball player, and an American whose dark hair marks his ancestry.

"En Mis Ojos no Hay Dias": This is by Judith Ortis Cofer, a Puerto Rican poet. She writes about her father's madness. Much of the understanding must come from an understanding of the context/culture in which her father was raised: rural and macho.

"From My Grandmother": Jo Whitehorse Cochran, of Lakota/Norwegian descent, writes about her grandmother and the spiritual gifts that that have been left to her.

"How Grandmother Spider Brought the Light": Paula Gunn Allen, a Pueblo woman, retells the story of how fire was brought to her people. Many animals try, but only Grandmother Spider is successful, for she accepted that she would be burned in the process, and planned for the pain.

"It Happened that Day": This is by Carmen Naranjo. The playmate of a young girl discovers her book of cutouts—pictures from magazines of what the little girl will look like when she grows up. The last picture was cut from the class's copy of *Snow White*, a crime for which the whole class was punished. The narrator is so angry the he/she ends the friendship.

"Juan Bobo": Juan Bobo stories are from Puerto Rico. In most of these stories Juan's mischief is balanced by a sort of wisdom. The story we used is a New York version in which he is a disobedient child who seems to have few redeeming qualities. He disobeys his mother by letting the pig go to church and piercing the baby's soft spot with a pin.

"Mike Fink Trying to Scare Mrs. Crockett": This is a rural/backwoods folktale, written in a thick dialect. Mike Fink dresses up as a bear, trying to scare Davy Crockett's shrew of a wife.

"Napa, California": This poem by Ana Castillo is about the Mexican migrant workers in California. The poem is in both English and Spanish—as the workers speak in the latter, surrounded by English words that describe their lives.

"Nikki Rosa": This poem is by Nikki Giovanni, an African American woman. Most of the poem is a description of her childhood. which she remembers being as happy, but which [White] biographers will always describe as hard, because of being African American and because her family did not have indoor toilets.

"Once to Run": This poem by Ron Welburn chronicles the disintegration of the Native American through the metaphor of running/being hounded.

The Devil Woman: A Mexican folktale about a man who gives a ride to a woman the night before his wedding. The woman is actually the devil, who scratches the man and throws him off his horse. His bride-to-be breaks off the wedding.

The People Could Fly: This is an African American folktale, retold by Virginia Hamilton, in which slaves are badly treated by a cruel overseer. Some of the slaves learn to fly away from their pain, whereas others remain behind.

"The Proof": This is by Rey Rosa. In it a young boy tries to test the existence of God by killing the family's canary. Their maid, seeing the empty cage, replaces the canary.

"The Rat in the Wall": This Chinese tale is about a man who cheats the workers who built his house. The workers, in turn, write curses on the beams of the house. The house remains haunted until a monster rat carries off the father, who can return only after his family has righted his wrongs.

"Theme for English B": Langston Hughes' poem serves as a response to his white instructor's request to write a page "about you." He finds that he cannot write about being Black and still assume that a White person will understand the experience.

"Traveling Through the Dark": This pastoral poem by William Stafford is about a man who, when traveling in his car, finds a deer just recently hit by another car. With his hands, he can feel a still-living baby moving inside the doe.

"Watering Trough": This is by Maxine Kumin. In it an old Victorian bathtub is now used as a watering trough for animals. The author pictures "our naked forbears" in what is now a rather pastoral environment.

"Welcome to the Human Heart": In this work by Janet Frame, a visitor to the Natural Science Museum in Philadelphia observes an elementary school class that is being shown some snakes. The museum attendant, careless of the teacher's terror, makes her hold the snake, and the teacher loses her composure in front of the class. The story is named because of the human heart exhibit the visitor would like to see.

"Yellow Woman": In this poem by Genevieve Lim-Jue, the "daughter of two worlds" struggles to "embrace one." The two worlds could be both China and the United States; the poem is both a personal and a historical narrative.

References

Amir, Y. (1982). Social assimilation or cultural mosaic? In J. Lynch, C. Modgil, & S. Modgil (Eds.), *Education for cultural diversity convergence and divergence: Cultural diversity and the schools* (Vol. 1, pp. 23–26). London: The Falmer Press.

Anderson, W. (1996). *The face of glory: Creativity, consciousness, and civilization.* London: Bloomsbury.

Applebee, A. N. (1990). *Literature instruction in American schools.* (Report Series 1.4). Albany, NY: National Research Center on Literature Teaching and Learning.

Applebee, A. N. (1991). *A study of high school literature anthologies.* (Report Series 1.5). Albany, NY: Center for the Learning and Teaching of Literature.

Bakhtin, M. (1994). *The Dialogic Imagination: Four essays by M. M. Bakhtin.* Austin, TX. University of Texas Press.

Banks, J. A. (1981). *Education in the 80's: Multiethnic education.* Washington, DC: National Education Association.

Banks, J. A. (1987). *Teaching strategies for ethnic studies* (4th ed.). Boston: Allyn and Bacon.

Banks, J. A. (1993a). Multicultural education: Characteristics and goals. In J. Banks & C. A. McGee Banks (Eds.), *Multicultural education: Issues and perspectives* (2nd ed., pp. 3–27). Boston: Allyn and Bacon.

Banks, J. A. (1993b). Approaches to multicultural curriculum reform. In J. Banks & C. A. McGee Banks (Eds.), *Multicultural education: Issues and perspectives* (2nd ed., pp. 195–214). Boston: Allyn and Bacon.

Banks, J. A. (1994). *An introduction to multicultural education.* Needham Hgts, MA: Allyn and Bacon.

Berleant, A. (1991). *Art and engagement.* Philadelphia: Temple University Press.

Chomsky, N. (1976). *Syntactic structures.* Paris: Mouton de Gruyter.

Damen, L. (1987). The communication and culture riddle. In (Ed.), *Culture learning: The fifth dimension in the language classroom* (pp. 73–96). Reading, MA: Addison-Wesley.

Dasenbrock, R. W. (1992). Teaching multicultural literature. In (Ed.), *Understanding others: Cultural and cross-cultural studies in the teaching of literature* (pp. 207–229). Urbana, IL: National Council of Teachers of English.

Dollerup, C. (1990). The Copenhagen studies on reader response. *Siegner Periodicum Zur Internationalen Empirischen Litteraturwissenschaft, 9*(2), 413–436.

Eck, D. L. (1993). *Encountering God: A spiritual journey from Bozeman to Benares.* Boston: Beacon Press.

Frye, N. (1957). *The anatomy of criticism.* Princeton, NJ: Princeton University Press.

Frye, N. (1991). *The double vision: Language and meaning in religion.* Toronto: Toronto University Press.

Gilroy, P. (1992). Cultural studies and ethnic absolutism. In L. Grossberg, C. Nelson and P. Treichler (Eds.), *Cultural studies* (pp. 187–198). New York: Routledge.

Goodenough, W. (1964). Cultural anthropology and linguistics. In D. Hymes (Ed.), *Language in culture and society* (pp. 36–39). New York: Harper & Row.

Grinter, R. (1992). Multicultural or antiracist education? The need to chose. In J. Lynch, C. Modgil, & S. Modgil (Eds.), *Education for cultural diversity convergence and divergence: Cultural diversity and the schools* (Vol. 1, pp. 95–111). London: The Falmer Press.

Hall, S. (1980). Cultural studies: Two paradigms. *Media, culture and society, 2*(5), 57–72.

Heath, S. B. (1983). *Ways with words: Language, life and work in communities and classrooms.* Cambridge, MA: Cambridge University Press.

Jordan, S., & Purves, A. C. (1993). *Issues in the responses of students to culturally diverse texts: A preliminary study* (Report No. 7.3). Albany, NY: Research Center on Literature and Teaching.

Lynch, J. (1986). *Multicultural education: Principles and practice.* Boston: Routledge & Kegan Paul.

Mayor, F. (1988, November). The world decade for cultural development. *The Courier, 41*(11), 5–6.

Miller, S. S., & McCaskill, B. (1993). *Multicultural literature and literaries: Making space for differences.* Albany, NY: State University of New York Press.

Nieto, S. (1992). *Affirming diversity: The sociopolitical context of multicultural education.* White Plains, NY: Longman.

Poole, M., & Sachs, J. (1992). Social assimilation or cultural mosaic. In J. Lynch, C. Modgil, & S. Modgil (Eds.), *Education for cultural diversity convergence and divergence: Cultural diversity and the schools* (Vol. 1, pp. 37–51). London: The Falmer Press.

Purves, A. C. (1973). *Literature education in ten countries: An empirical study.* Stockholm: Almqvist and Wiksell.

Ravitch, D. (1990a). Multiculturalism: E pluribus plures. *The American Scholar, 59,* 337–354.

Ravitch, D. (1990b). Diversity and democracy. *American Educator, 14,* 16–20, 46–48.

Richards, I. A. (1929). *Practical criticism: A study of literary judgment.* New York: Harcourt Brace.

Rosenblatt, L. (1978). *The reader, the text, and the poem.* Cambridge, MA: Harvard University Press.

Rosenblatt, L. (1994). *The reader, the text, and the poem: The transactional theory of the literary work.* Carbondale, IL: Southern Illinois University Press.

Said, E. (1983). *The world, the text, and the critic.* Cambridge, MA: Harvard University Press.

Said, E. (1994). *Culture and imperialism.* New York: Knopf.

Scharme, S. (1989). *citizens: A chronicle of the French Revolution.* New York: Knopf.

Squire, J. R. (1963). *The responses of adolescents to four short stories.* Urbana, IL: National Council of Teachers of English.

Super, C. M., & Harkness, S. (1986). The developmental niche: A conceptualization at the interface of child and culture. *Journal of Behavioral Development, 9*(4), 545–569.

Super, C. M., & Harkness, S. (1993). The developmental niche: Implications for children's literacy development. In L. Elderling & P. Leseman (Eds.), *Early intervention and culture: Preparation for literacy. The interface between theory and practice* (pp. 37–52). Netherlands: National commission for UNESCO.

Triandis, H. C. (1980). Introduction to handbook of cross-cultural psychology. In H. C. Triandis & W. W. Wilson (Eds.), *Handbook of cross-cultural psychology: Perspectives* (Vol. 1, pp. 3–35). Boston: Allyn and Bacon.

Williams, R. (1961). *The long revolution.* London: Chatto and Windus.

Williams, R. (1977). *Marxism and literature.* Oxford, England: Oxford University Press.

Author Index

❧ ◆ ☙

Subject Index

&ztwixt; ◆ &ztwixt;

About the Authors

❧ ◆ ❧

Gladys I. Cruz holds a BA in elementary education and an MA in education with a specialization in Bilingual Education. She works as a Research Assistant for the National Research Center on English Learning and Achievement at State University of New York at Albany. She also works as a consultant for the New York State Education Department, Office of Bilingual Education, where she has developed Guidelines for Two-Way Bilingual Education programs in that state and has aided in the production of a statewide video of Two-Way programs. Her research interests include bilingual and multicultural education. She is conducting her dissertation study in a Two-Way Bilingual Education program at the middle school level.

Sarah Jordan received her doctorate in education at the University of Albany. Her research focus has been in the areas of multicultural literature and portfolio assessment, both at the high school level. She has lectured and conducted workshops on both topics in the United States and abroad. Currently, she teaches in the Alternative Education Department at Wachusett Regional High School in Holden, Massachusetts.

Steve Ostrowski holds a BA in English Literature and an MFA in Creative Writing and has taught both high school English and college composition. He is currently completing his dissertation in the Department of Educational Theory and Practice at the State University of New York at Albany, where he is a research assistant with the National Research Center on English Learning and Achievement. His areas of specialization include Composition, English Education, and the Teaching of Writing. In addition to his academic writings, Ostrowski has published poetry and fiction in literary journals throughout North America.

José Meléndez holds a BA in Philosophy and Literature, and an M. Ed in Reading and Language teaching at the middle school level. He has a rich background as a professor and administrator in a variety of undergraduate and graduate teacher

107

training programs in New York State and Puerto Rico. He is currently a doctoral candidate in the Curriculum and Instruction specialization in the Department of Educational Theory and Practice of the State University of New York at Albany. There, he also works as a research assistant for the National Research Center on English Learning and Achievement. As part of his doctoral work, he has conducted extensive research in the areas of multicultural literature, interdisciplinary curricula, first and second language literacy acquisition, and educational and language policies affecting students from linguistic minorities. At present, he is working on his doctoral dissertation: A comparative study of the approaches to the study of culture in the high school literature curricula of New York State and the Commonwealth of Puerto Rico.

Alan C. Purves—December 14, 1931–December 31, 1996. Formerly Director of the Center for Writing and Literacy, and project leader for multicultural literature for the National Literature Center, Dr. Purves was Professor Emeritus of Education and Humanities at SUNY Albany. While a specialist in literature, composition, and assessment, he taught English in elementary and secondary schools, as well as in colleges and universities. He was a former president of the National Council of Teachers of English (NCTE). For many years, he worked with the International Association for the Evaluation of Educational Achievement (IEA), first as Chairman of the Study of Written Composition and later as IEA Chairman. His work with the IEA made him a leader in international studies comparing education and achievement. He had recently edited the two-volume Encyclopedia of English Studies and Language Arts, and his most recent publication was a collaborative work on portfolios in the literature classroom. Dr. Purves' book, *The Web of Text and the Web of God*, which explores religion and cyberspace, will be published in the fall of 1997.